enchanted
CRYSTAL
MAGIC

About the Author

Pamela Chen is the creator of the Crystal Unicorn Tarot, a self-published deck for rainbow, Unicorn, and pastel loving readers. She is also the creator of the *Witchling Academy Tarot*, published by Llewellyn. Her passion and purpose is to help spiritual entrepreneurs create a heart-centered, lucrative online business that stands out and sells out. She has also co-founded 7 Figure Luxe Goddess Mastermind, a twelve-month experience for high-achieving leaders to activate their prosperity codes. When Pamela is not playing with her chickens or slinging cards, she loves to read paranormal romance, travel the world, and eat spicy Cheeto puffs. Connect with Pamela on Instagram: @pamelaunicorn.

enchanted
CRYSTAL
MAGIC

Spells, Grids & Potions to Manifest Your Desires

PAMELA CHEN

Llewellyn Publications • Woodbury, Minnesota

Bad Moon Apothecary

376 Garcia St.
Santa Fe, NM 87501
(505)670-6659

There's a little witch in all of us

FIRST EDITION
First Printing, 2021

Cover design by Kevin R. Brown
Interior female chakra figure and chakra figure in the color insert © Mary Ann Zapalac.
    Other art by the Llewellyn Art Department

Llewellyn Publications is a registered trademark of Llewellyn
    Worldwide Ltd.

Library of Congress Cataloging-in-Publication Data
Names: Chen, Pamela, author.
Title: Enchanted crystal magic : spells, grids & potions to manifest your desires / Pamela
    Chen.
Description: First edition. | Woodbury, MN: Llewellyn Worldwide, Ltd, [2021] | Includes
    bibliographical references and index. | Summary: "This book helps you start your own
    crystal enchanter practice to improve your love life, manifest more money, heal emotional
    wounds, and connect with your true sparkly self" —Provided by publisher.
Identifiers: LCCN 2021029178 (print) | LCCN 2021029179 (ebook) | ISBN 9780738767161
    (paperback) | ISBN 9780738767246 (ebook)
Subjects: LCSH: Crystals—Miscellanea. | Precious stones—Miscellanea. | Magic.
Classification: LCC BF1442.C78 C54 2021 (print) | LCC BF1442.C78
    (ebook) | DDC 133.3/22—dc23
LC record available at https://lccn.loc.gov/2021029178
LC ebook record available at https://lccn.loc.gov/2021029179

Llewellyn Publications
A Division of Llewellyn Worldwide Ltd.
2143 Wooddale Drive
Woodbury, MN 55125-2989
www.llewellyn.com

Printed in the United States of America

Other Work by Pamela Chen

Witchling Academy Tarot

Dedication

To my mentor, inspiration, and business partner Leeza. Grateful for all the times you ask me, "What does this mean?" in my writing, and for overflowing your trash bin with my manuscripts.

Contents

Contents

Exercises

Disclaimer

The information provided in this book in not a substitution for consulting a medical health care professional. All the information in this book, including the information related to mental health, physical health, medical conditions, crystals, and treatments, is for educational, informational, and entertainment purposes only. Please consult a health care professional before starting any crystal or essential oil treatments. For diagnosis or treatment of any medical condition, readers are advised to seek the services of a competent medical professional.

While best efforts have been used in preparing this book, neither the author nor the publisher shall be held liable or responsible to any person or entity with respect to any loss or damages caused, or alleged to have been caused, directly or indirectly, by the information contained herein. Every situation is different, and the advice and strategies contained in this book may not be suitable for your situation.

In the following pages you will find recommendations for the use of certain herbs, essential oils, and blends. If you are allergic to any of these items, please refrain from use. Do your own research before using an essential oil. Each body reacts differently to herbs, essential oils, and other items, so results may vary person to person. Essential oils are potent; use care when handling them. Always dilute essential oils before placing them on your skin, and make sure to do a patch test on your skin before use. Never ingest essential oils. Some herbal remedies can react with prescription or over-the-counter medications in adverse ways. If you are on medication or have health issues, please do not ingest any herbs without first consulting a qualified practitioner.

Some crystals are toxic, harmful, or poisonous if left on the skin. Other crystals are toxic, harmful, or poisonous if ingested in any way. Always do your research before handling a crystal, especially if you have never worked with that specific crystal before. If you are allergic to any of the crystals suggested in this book, please refrain from use. If you use the direct method when making crystal potions, be extremely cautious, do your research, and make sure the crystal is nontoxic before ingesting crystal-infused water. To err on the side of caution, use the indirect method when making crystal potions. Never ingest a crystal.

Introduction

The first time I actively tried to use my magic was after watching *The Craft*, a pretty well-known movie filled with powerful witches. It was the nineties and I was in elementary school. Energy and magic have always been a part of my life, but that movie inspired me to put more intention and focus into the magic. At that time, I decided to call in the elements to test my so-called powers. I sat on a high branch of my mango tree, closed my eyes, raised my arms into the sky, and called the element of air, just like they did in the movie. *Whoosh!* A blast of wind blew through the branches and into my hair, sending it flying. *Wow*, I thought, *I have magic!* However, after performing the "Light as a Feather, Stiff as a Board" ritual and trying to make my pencil levitate, the magical experiments faded out as "real life" got in the way. I'm grateful that I eventually found my way back to magic as a young adult.

When my intuition nudged me back into exploring this mystical craft, I started gathering all the books and tools I could find, and eventually I took lessons from magical mentors and immersed myself in energy healing modalities. Luckily, there has been a massive shift in spiritual awakening in the twenty-first century, and now mysticism is very much mainstream. The movement to this acceptance has allowed me to tap into the wisdom and knowledge of magic, healing, and manifesting even more. Throughout the years, I've studied, taught, and embodied many magical beliefs. I currently share my magic and modalities by teaching online courses to a great collective of students, who I call my Unicorns because they are all so sparkly and filled with magic. I have to admit, unicorns and crystals are connected for me. They both top the list of my favorite enchanted things.

It wasn't really until I started to connect to crystals and began to devote myself to the Crystal Enchantment path that success and fulfillment started appearing in my life. It had seemed like something was missing from my spiritual practice, and I felt like I was always searching for more. What shifted my belief in crystals was when my best friend, Yayoi, gifted me a citrine tower. At that time, I was starting a magical online business and trying to make it successful. She told me that the citrine was for abundance and luck with my business, so I put it on my computer. That week, new clients started appearing out of nowhere! "Oh my Goddess," we said. "It's the crystal!"

After that, we were both believers in crystal magic. We traveled around the world, going to crystal shows in places like Denver, Japan, Taiwan, and Arizona. We went wherever we could go to find sparkly crystals! One day, out of the blue, we decided to sell crystals on Instagram and opened up a crystal boutique called Luna Prosperity.

This decision shifted my entire life. The magic of crystals definitely leveled me up. Through our crystal business, I was recognized in the coaching industry as a crystal expert and was able to help our Unicorn clients find love, manifest more money, and heal their emotional and physical pain. We have even had some celebrity clients who we worked with to help bring in good crystal vibes. They included a famous golfer, a Japanese model, and the rapper Lil Jon, whose house we placed crystals inside of for abundance.

Through my own personal experiences with crystals, my years of research, and my clients' success stories, I have so much magical knowledge and so many tips to share with you. I even incorporated a full module on crystals, their magic, and their healing properties within the High Magic

Certification Program and Spiritual Business Course that I co-founded with Leeza Robertson.

The spells, practices, and rituals that I have shared with my clients and students—and that I now share with you—are easy to perform and perfect for a crystal beginner diving into the craft. I'm hoping that by presenting it this way, you also will experience the magic of the crystals and be able to use the wisdom from this book to help you achieve your goals and live your best sparkly life.

If you are a complete newbie to magic and crystals, don't worry. I believe that everyone has inner magic and can activate and claim their Crystal Enchanter powers. Anyone can create a practice that brings balance, happiness, and fulfillment to their life. You may need to experiment with your mystical craft for a while before you find your flow, but working with crystal energies to heal, manifest, and shift your life is completely available to you. It just takes practice and a commitment to exploring and playing with your craft to see what works and doesn't work for you.

Everyone is vibrating at a specific energetic frequency, so working with crystals will be different for each person. My suggestion is to start a crystal journal or spell book and document your magical adventure. Keep your mind open and be ready to learn. Approach each exercise, spell, and practice with fresh eyes. Try everything and see what works for you. Make adjustments if needed. Cultivate a unique Crystal Enchanter practice that will work for you, a magical practice that will bring excitement and happiness into your everyday life.

At the beginning of my crystal journey, I could not feel the energy of crystals. During a holistic fair, the ladies around me held some crystal bracelets, exclaiming how powerful they were and how they felt the energy. Being curious about magic, I picked up one of the bracelets and attempted to feel the energy for myself. Guess what? I felt nothing. So if you are not able to feel crystal energy or your own inner intuitive connection to crystals at this moment, don't be discouraged! If you continue to practice your Crystal Enchanter craft, follow the exercises in this book, and keep handling crystals, you will be able to feel the energy, communicate with your crystals, and utilize them in so many amazing ways.

When you connect with the Crystal Enchanter within, you will:

- Be aware of the energy of your crystal and the messages that are being shared with you.
- Be open to the wonders and miracles that crystal magic can bring into your life.
- Be open to exploring mysteries and knowledge from the crystal realm.

- Allow the energies of the crystal to support, guide, and heal you.

Are you ready to immerse yourself in the magic of crystals and say yes to discovering your Crystal Enchanter self? Then let's dive in and see what sparkly lessons you will learn in the pages of this book.

In chapter 1, you will learn what crystals are and how to connect with their energies. We will travel back in time to discover how ancient civilizations and royalty used crystals. You will learn more about the foundations of magic and spells and kick off your Crystal Enchanter practice in chapter 2. Chapter 3 is a powerful chapter, as it will introduce you to crystal color magic in relation to your seven main chakras. Color magic is the foundation of many spells, and understanding the energy of the colors can also help you choose a crystal to work with quickly. What to do with your crystals once you have chosen them is discussed in chapter 4. I also share many tips and tricks about how I care for my magical crystal collection. In chapters 5 through chapter 10, you learn all the components of your Crystal Enchanter craft! Each chapter focuses on a specific energy in your life that you need to enhance or call in. Three potent crystals are selected for each chapter, along with a message from the crystal collective that I have divinely channeled. A powerful meditation, spell, or ritual is also shared for your work with the crystals. With the beginner Crystal Enchanter in mind, the crystals I discuss in each chapter are budget friendly and easy to find and purchase. In chapter 11, you will learn how to create and activate magical crystal grids. Chapter 12 will teach you how to make different crystal potions and how to use each type in your magical practices. Finally, in chapter 13, you will learn how to create your own magical crystal spells, because a Crystal Enchanter has to know how to create their own spells, right?!

My wish for you is that you are able to open your heart and energy to the crystals and claim your unique magic, to fully integrate this craft into your daily practices for inspiration and healing, and to create a reality that allows your authentic Crystal Enchanter self to sparkle! So take out your crystal spell book or a favorite journal—let's start your adventure!

EXERCISE
Crystal Energy Discovery

This is a simple magical exercise that will help you discover how you connect to crystal energy. First, find a crystal to connect with. It can be any crystal in your collection. Then find a place where you won't be disturbed and can sit comfortably. Close your eyes and focus on the crystal that is resting in the palm of your hands. Take three long, deep breaths, focusing intently on your breathing, and then shift your focus to the crystal.

Investigate the crystal with your senses. How does it feel? Is it rough, smooth, or a little bit of both? What color is it? What is the temperature of the crystal? Is it cold, hot, or warm? Is it heavy or light? How does the crystal feel in your hands? Bring your awareness to your heart connection with the crystal. How does this crystal make you feel emotionally? Do you feel happy right now? Are you calm? Or are you feeling something else? Keep investigating your crystal and feel love for your crystal. When you are ready, thank your crystal and open your eyes.

If you are able to answer the questions that I asked above, congratulations! You have felt the crystal's energy. If you just blanked and got nothing, don't worry, you just need more practice, and it will come!

In your crystal journal, write down what you discovered. You can try this exercise with multiple different crystals to see if there is a pattern. You will have your own unique way of figuring out the crystal's energies, and it is up to you to discover this magic.

Chapter 1
The Sparkly World of Crystals

For new and obsessed crystal lovers, it's important to know the origins of crystal magic beliefs and why many people from the past and present are so fascinated with these glittering gems. Crystals have been connected to humankind for thousands and thousands of years. During this chapter, we will go on a magical journey to discover what crystals are and learn about their history.

What Are Crystals?

For those who are not familiar, crystals are minerals that are formed naturally in the earth. They are created when liquid cools down and hardens. One of the major differences between a rock and crystal is that as the liquid solidifies, a crystal has a repeating atomic structure while a rock does not. The pattern and arrangement of a certain crystal is always going to be the same on a molecular level, but no two crystals will look exactly the same to the human eye. Although crystals and rocks are formed differently, they both contain powerful earth magic. Working with both can be beneficial to your crystal practice, and that is why I have also tumbled in some rocks and suggested them for your magical collection.

It should also be noted that crystals can be created in laboratories, but I tend not to work with 100 percent manmade crystals because my intention is to tap into the natural energies of the earth. If you are called to work with manmade crystals, that is fine. There are no hard rules on what you can or cannot do with crystals. It is totally up to you! Some of my favorite crystals are partly altered and heat treated, like aqua aura quartz, which is quartz coated with metal fumes such as gold or silver.

During my experiences working with crystals in healing modalities such as Reiki, I have found that crystals positively interact with your energy field, chakras, and aura. They have vibrational energy that positively interacts with the aura and chakras to help balance and heal the physical, mental, emotional, and spiritual bodies.

They are powerful vibrational tools that can help you achieve your goals, relieve stress, activate intuition, and so much more. They are able to enhance the energy in and around you. These gorgeous gems from the earth are amazing to meditate with and use in magic.

Crystal History

Crystals have been a tool for healing and magic since ancient times. Throughout history, royalty and rulers adorned themselves with crystals. Kings and queens surrounded themselves and their homes with rubies, diamonds, emeralds, and more. This was not only for the beauty and the opulence of the mineral, but for the protection and enchanting properties of the crystals.

The ancient Greeks labeled these magical gems *krýstallos*, meaning clear ice.[1] Sounds an awful lot like *crystal*, right? Many of the words that we use today regarding the sparkly gems came from the ancient Greeks. For example, amethyst means "not drunken" and was created as an amulet to help with hangovers and to prevent the wearer from getting too intoxicated. Quartz crystals were used by many groups of ancient people like Greeks, Romans, and the Egyptians as talismans.[2]

....

1. Merriam-Webster, s.v. "crystal (n.)," accessed March 23, 2021, https://www.merriam-webster.com/dictionary/crystal.

2. Chamberlain, *Wicca Crystal Magic*, chap. 1.

These minerals were also coveted in Asian countries. In ancient China, jade was considered the most preferred and valued gem. To the Chinese, jade was a symbol of purity, sacredness, wisdom, and beauty. Jade was made into jewelry, instruments, talismans, and even armor for the burials of emperors. In Chinese, the word jade translates to "heavenly stone." Ancient India also mentioned the use of stones. Diamonds, rubies, and emeralds were very popular. There is a traditional Hindu belief that rubies were worshipped because they were recognized as the gemstone of the sun, so the wearer would gain blessings from the sun.

As you can see, crystal magic is embedded into history. It probably came to be this way because ancient civilizations sensed some kind of power and connection to the crystals and picked them up to use them as protective magical tools like amulets. As the practice of crystal magic evolved and began to be included in rituals and religion, it became a tool that is revered and used to bring abundant blessings.[3]

For a time the knowledge and wisdom of crystal magic was lost. But during the beginning of the New Age era, around the 1980s, crystals quietly surfaced again. Crystals began to work their way into energy healing modali-

---

3. Cunningham, *Cunningham's Encyclopedia of Crystal, Gem & Metal Magic*, 1.

ties as a complementary magical tool, and many holistic and spiritual practitioners began incorporating the healing energies of crystals into their work. From there, the magic of crystals was widely shared, and now many magical practitioners also play the role of Crystal Enchanter, integrating the energies of these stones into their rituals, spells, and healing journey.

Modern Crystal Times

I am very grateful for the rise of the spiritual movement in the New Age culture, which has allowed us to rediscover the magic of the crystals. We now have incredible access to crystals and can even buy them online from anywhere in the world. This allows anyone to learn how to use their energies for healing.

Fascinatingly enough, crystals are even used in technology! Ultrasounds, computer chips, sonar, and digital watches have a little quartz crystal in the devices. For those who didn't know, the quartz helps to keep an accurate time and regulate the movement of the watch or clock. Aren't all the different things these gems provide magical?

Since crystals have hit the mainstream, you can now casually bring them up in a conversation and most people will know what they are. As spiritual well-being and consciousness have risen around the world, so have crystals.

I recently read that famous celebrities are coming out of the crystal closet and sharing their gems, including Victoria Beckham, who always keeps crystals backstage at her fashion shows. Celebrity fitness instructor Taryn Toomey, whose client list includes Jennifer Aniston, embedded clear quartz, amethyst, and rose quartz beneath the floors of her workout studio for high vibes. And then there's Adele, who claims to perform better when she has her crystals.[4] As shared previously, one of my crystal clients is Lil Jon, who consulted me and my business partner about various crystals for his home. We were able to help him bring crystal energy and good vibes into his fabulous home.

Crystals and You

You might be thinking, *Wow, look at the amazing uses of these crystals. But I'm not making a computer or putting in new floors, so what can I do with them?* Well, good thing you picked up this book, because we're about to go on an epic crystal adventure! The main rule of this adventure is to do what makes you feel happy. If you want to sleep with your crystal, then do it. If you want to carry it in your pocket, then do that. If you have no idea what to do with crystals, then keep reading and prepare to sparkle and heal with your gems.

....

4. Studeman, "Are You Obsessed with Crystals, Too?"

The way that we will be working with crystals in this book is by using these minerals to raise your vibrational energy, balance your emotions, and attract what you truly desire. Adding crystals into your daily rituals will deepen and enhance your spiritual practice. Crystals can help you energetically align with the things that you want to call in by working and raising your energies. They can also protect you and release blockages to help you reach your goals.

One of the best ways to work with crystals is to figure out the specific one that you need for your situation and then to carry that crystal around with you. Make sure the crystal is small enough to fit in your pocket or bag; leave the bigger ones around your house and office so they can provide their magical energy there. In the next two chapters, I'll help you learn how to find and choose the best crystal for you, based on your current needs and desires.

Crystal Tip
Carrying Crystals

The best way to gain good vibes from your magical gems during the day, when you are out and about, is to carry a small tumbled stone with you. A tumbled stone is a crystal that has been through a tumbling machine. The machine smooths out the crystal so it looks polished. Tumbled stones are usually smaller in size and are perfect for your pocket or your bag. If you're going to be putting the stone somewhere it could get scratched or dirty, make sure to put it in a velvet bag or something similar first, especially if it is a more expensive stone that you cherish.

Crystals work best when they are touching your skin, so if it's possible, I would suggest you to have skin-to-crystal contact. For you gorgeous crystal lovers who wear bras, just tuck one (or three) in your bra and you are ready for an awesome day. Make sure that when you undress later, you remember your gems are still in your pocket or bra! You don't want the stone to accidentally clatter to the ground and chip. Unfortunately, this is something that happens to me all the time. You can still use the crystal if it's chipped, just make sure you don't get cut when handling it. If you feel ready to retire the crystal, store it in a safe space, gift it, or bury it in dirt.

Clients have told me how much happier and more confident they feel during the day when they have their crystals with them. Many often remark that they feel naked without them.

Chapter 2
Crystal Spells and Magic

Chapter 2 is a must-read chapter before you move on. In this chapter, I'll be talking about what crystal spells and magic are. Reading through this section can help you understand the foundation of crystal practice and how to get the most out of the magic in this book. Whether you are a newbie or someone already working with crystals, I suggest you try out and practice the spells provided in this book, then go on to craft your own.

In this chapter, I will be sharing my tips on spell work so that you can have a deeper connection to the spells in the Crystal Enchanter practice. Everyone is unique and will have their way of practicing magic and working with spells. Take what resonates with you from my teachings and feel free to create your own Crystal Enchanter practice. As shared previously, you will learn how to create your own magical spells in chapter 13.

As a Crystal Enchanter, we utilize spells because they are a powerful way to focus magic and intention. Spells are a way to manifest desires into reality. When you are doing a spell, you are consciously and subconsciously shifting your physical world. You are making your thoughts and ideas real. Magic is something that we can't see or hold in our hands, but by combining it with tangible objects like crystals, we can touch and work with it in reality.

Now, let's use the magic of crystals to change our lives, to change the world, and to bring some sparkly wishes into reality.

What Is Magic?

Magic is everywhere around you and in you. You are already working with magic daily. Have you ever thought hard about wanting something and suddenly someone surprised you with it? Have you dreamed of a specific scene and then had it happen in real life? Have you done a tarot reading for someone and had them confirm that what you said was true? Have you wished upon a star and come one step closer to your dreams? That is all magic.

You do not need to be of a specific religion or have a certain belief system to use magic. No matter what your beliefs are, no matter what your religion is, you can activate your magic! And in this book, we will be using crystal spells to do so.

My Crystal Enchanter's definition of magic is "using the energies that are within you and surrounding you to bring your thoughts and desires into reality." Everyone is magical; you are born programmed with magic. If you aren't feeling magical, that's probably because you aren't aware of how magic feels. This could be because you haven't been taught about what it is. There was no magic class in the school that I went to, and we had no Hogwarts in Hawaii, where I grew up. Lucky for you, learning how to be aware of your energies and magic is very simple once you learn about it. All it takes is reading books like this and lots of practice. Both are important. Reading and learning about energies and magic is the first step, but combining it with the practical exercises is what will help you understand it more fully and create the magical life you desire.

What Are Spells?

For the sake of this book and my work as a Crystal Enchanter, I see spells as a tool to help people focus on a specific intention and to bring wishes into reality by doing a physical activity. After every crystal description in chapters 5 through 10, I will be sharing a spell for that specific energy. When you are doing the spell, your focus should be entirely on the task you are doing and the thing that you want to call into your life. That is very potent magic. Our minds and thoughts are very powerful, and spells are tools to help you amplify the energy to attract what you want. Of course, you don't need crystals or anything else to manifest your wish; you can just do it with your energy and mindset. However, for myself and many others, working with crystals and other magical tools makes it easier to bridge the gap between thoughts and manifesting those thoughts into reality. Using magical tools can also help you manifest more quickly. When we are in the act of doing the spell, we create a vortex of energy that connects us directly to the Universe so that the wish or desire that we are asking for is heard loud and clear. Your desires tend to appear faster because every step of your spell will allow you to be even more profoundly focused on your intention.

Spells are a sequence of activities that you do one at a time. Spells are charms, incantations, enchantments, and magical formulas that are created to help you take action. People practice spells when they want to change or enhance their life. A spell can be anything you want it to be. It can be as long or as short as you want, and you can use any magical tools you choose. There isn't a right or wrong way to do a spell. In fact, sometimes I just say some words while I stir my morning coffee or tea!

I would suggest not repeating the same spell until at least a month has passed. From my Crystal Enchanter experience, it is better to leave it alone and let the magic work than to rush it. If you perform the same spell too soon, before it has been manifested, you could be blocking the first spell's manifestations from coming into your life.

Setting Intentions

The most powerful thing in your spells are your intentions. Intentions are essential in crafting a crystal spell. Intentions are potent because they incorporate your thoughts, feelings, and beliefs. What powers spells, rituals, crystals, and other magical items are your intentions. Most people don't know how to set a powerful intention for instant manifestation. So, before we start creating any spells or rituals, let's make sure that our intentions are on point.

First of all, when writing an intention, write it as if it has already happened. For example, instead of saying, "I wish I had _____," you want to say, "I already have _____." This is to train your mind and energy to be comfortable with that reality and to help you shift toward your goal faster. For an extra boost, you can also add gratitude and love to start your intention, such as, "I am so grateful and happy that I have _____."

Your intention has to be as specific as possible. Write a whole paragraph about it if you'd like. The more details you share, the more the Universe will understand exactly what you are calling in and send it your way. For example, if you are manifesting a car, you would intend, "I am so happy and grateful that I have bought my dream car within my budget. I have found the perfect new, white BMW 3 Series with chocolate interior leather seats."

Your intention has to be believable. You have to believe that this can happen to you in real life. What I mean is, you can manifest anything you want, and there is no limit to magic. However, the one thing that may be limiting you is yourself. For example, let's say you want to stretch your comfort zone a little wider and intend for something a little more, but you manifest something extreme, like buying a Ferrari the next day. You consciously and sub-consciously will be thinking, *Psh, that can never happen*, and so it *won't* ever happen.

Intentions are more powerful when you attach a feeling to them and when you visualize them. When you imagine yourself already doing and being the person you want to be and having all the things you desire, it can convince the mind that you already have it because your mind does not know if it's real yet or not. That's why visualization and mindset exercises work—because your mind cannot distinguish between something you made up or a memory. It just knows that whatever you are thinking and believing is real life. When we remember a memory or a past event, it's usually because it's attached to a strong emotion. So what if you attach a strong, happy emotion to your intention? You will most likely see it manifest, because you already believe it is so. When we focus on the abundance of happiness and joy, that is when it starts flowing more our way, and our desires become a reality. So, visualize your intention and attach a strong, happy emotion to it as a basis for your spells.

And then let it go! After you have set your intention and done your spell for the day, let it go. Don't focus on how it'll come to you, when it will happen, or why it will appear in your life. All this thinking would just block your intentions from coming true and keep you stuck and worried. It is important to just forget about it and trust it will come your way.

I have shared with you a few magical keys to crafting the perfect intention that will help you manifest your desires. Just by using these techniques, your spells are almost guaranteed to come to fruition! Of course, there are no guarantees in magic or in life, but you know what I mean. I share a bit more about this later, in the chapter's Crystal Tip.

Sacred Space

Having a sacred space where you perform your crystal spells is very important. This sets the mood for your practice and lets your subconscious know that you are ready for the magic. Your sacred space doesn't have to be super elaborate for you to do magic there. No, it can be simple, just someplace where you and your magic won't be disturbed and where you feel comfortable. My sacred space is my office. I have a wooden drawer where I place all my spell work. I know that some of my students who have animals and children create spells in drawers so they can close the drawer to prevent their spell work from being knocked over.

Some magic casters love working with spells on their altars. An altar is just a dedicated space that you have decorated with items that help focus on the energy that you would like to call in, or a spiritual center where you can connect with your magical self. For example, you could have a mini altar in your home that focuses on love or money. This altar could be set up on your windowsill, the top of your dresser, or any other flat surface. Your altar might consist of a few crystals, candles, and tarot cards. Choose items that feel right to you.

Always cleanse your sacred space before starting your crystal spells or rituals so that you have positive energy surrounding you. You can use herbs like rosemary or lavender to do so, or, if you don't have any of that, imagine a white light shining brighter and brighter from your heart and filling up the space around you to cleanse every area of the room, including the corners. If you have been certified in energetic healing modalities like Reiki, you can also use that to clear the energy of the room.

Crystal Tip
Practice Makes Magic

When you practice your crystal-enhanced spells, it is not a guarantee that a spell will come true. There are many moving parts to magic, and that's why you should keep a spell book or journal to record your process. Think of casting spells like an experiment. Sometimes your first try will be a success, and sometimes it takes a few adjustments and tweaks before you are satisfied with your results. If your intention or wish does not come true, that is okay. Even though it did not come true, you are probably one step closer to your goal! There might be a few things you can adjust before trying the spell or ritual again after a month or two. Maybe your intention is not aligned with what you truly desire, or perhaps you have some thoughts and beliefs that need to be shifted and cleared before you can manifest the things that you want. Most of the time it is your belief or intention, not so much the magical tools.

Don't give up on your dreams. Keep going, but be flexible and aware of how the Universe is trying to guide you. You are given signs and inspiration every single day. Most of the time we ignore these signs because we do not know they are there. Instead of living in the past or trying to predict what will happen, focus on the present moment—on what is happening right now—so you are attuned to receiving these signs. You can intentionally ask for signs to show up, or you can look for some commons signs like:

- Angel numbers like 111, 222, etc. that you might see on a license plate or your digital clock.
- Feathers floating in front of you.
- Coins on the ground.
- Animals and insects that show up unexpectedly.
- A phrase that catches your attention in a song.

Also, your wish might still be coming, so be patient! Things may still be in the process of manifesting. Keep a positive mindset and positive energy, and continue to trust that your intention will show up in divine timing.

Crystal Enchanter Spells

There are six crystal-enhanced spells that I have crafted specifically for this book. All of these spells will include a crystal with a specific energy. In chapters 5 through 10, you will find the spells and the crystals that are needed for each spell, but you don't need to use only those crystals—you can use any crystals you desire. These magical spells have already been tested by myself or my clients and have had amazing results.

Have fun with the magic, spells, and crystals! When you manifest from a place of joy and fulfillment, it is easier to call in what you desire. If you don't know what you are doing with crystals and magic, don't worry. You will learn my Crystal Enchanter secrets in this book and be guided by spells already created for you. Take what resonates with you and leave the rest. You get to choose your unique path. You get to choose how you dictate your Crystal Enchanter practice.

Chapter 3
Crystal Color Magic

Color magic is one of the most powerful elements used in healing and magical practices, including spells. Each individual color has specific properties that attracts different energies into your life. It isn't a coincidence that crystals come in all different colors and embody a particular energy when it comes to healing, and that is why they are one of my favorite healing and focusing tools to use daily. They emit powerful energies and naturally work with our bodies to balance and heal.

Knowing color magic is one of the most important steps in helping you choose the right crystal. It's considered a must in my book because learning the magic behind each crystal's color will help you identify which crystal you need for your specific healing or situation. Even though each crystal has a deeper magical meaning, using color to select your crystal is a quick and easy way to find the energy you need to call upon. Keep in mind, choosing a crystal by color is only one of the magical ways of selecting the "right" crystal for the job. Other methods will be discussed throughout the later chapters of this book.

Crystal Color Magical Meanings

In this section, I describe the meanings of different crystal colors. While each color has a general magical meaning that most practitioners typically agree on, keep in mind that you are unique, so you may react to a color in a different way. Thus, it is important to experiment with crystal colors yourself and find what works best for you.

I will be discussing crystal connections to the chakras in this section as well. Refer to figure 1 for the positioning and colors of the chakras.

Red
Chakra: Root chakra
Crystals: Ruby, red calcite, garnet, red jasper, red aura
    quartz

Keywords: Prosperity, joy, masculinity, warmth, heat, desire, life, action, passion, lust, confidence, leadership, fertility

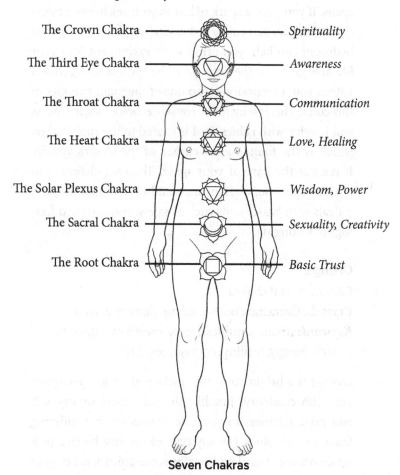

The Crown Chakra —————— *Spirituality*

The Third Eye Chakra —————— *Awareness*

The Throat Chakra —————— *Communication*

The Heart Chakra —————— *Love, Healing*

The Solar Plexus Chakra —————— *Wisdom, Power*

The Sacral Chakra —————— *Sexuality, Creativity*

The Root Chakra —————— *Basic Trust*

Seven Chakras

The color red is often associated with love, desire, and passion, and it is often used in attraction or seduction spells. If you need a spark of lust in your sex life or a boost in confidence, carrying a red crystal or putting it in your bedroom can help you bring some excitement into your life and give you the courage to be the sex god/goddess within you. Prosperity is also one of the main energies of this color. This is why many royals decorated their crowns and jewelry with rubies. Red is related to the root chakra, which is the foundational chakra of the chakra system. It rests at the base of your spine. The root chakra is in charge of your survival instincts and your confidence, and it deals with basic needs such as safety, comfort, and feelings of belonging.

Orange

Chakra: Sacral chakra

Crystals: Carnelian, orange calcite, sunstone, halite

Keywords: Heat, sunniness, spice, creativity, curiosity, luck, energy, healing, courage, fertility

Orange is a bright color that picks you up and energizes you with creativity! Just like the fruit itself, orange will add extra juiciness to your life. When you are suffering from writer's block (or any type of creative block), pick up an orange crystal and ask for some guidance. Let your crystal inspire you to create and have the courage to share it with the world. I always recommend carnelian to any-one who is feeling unsure of themselves or in a bit of a depression. An orange crystal can also help with fertil-ity issues and help you conceive. The color orange repre-sents the sacral chakra, which is the second chakra that sits right above your root chakra, near your lovely private parts. The sacral chakra works with your creative, sensual, and emotional self, dealing with emotional responses and your desires. Orange wants to remind you to love the life that you are living, enjoy the life you were given, and experience life to the fullest.

Yellow

Chakra: Solar plexus chakra

Crystals: Citrine, tiger's eye, apatite, yellow fluorite, amber, pyrite, copper, gold

Keywords: Joy, manifesting, clarity, abundance, confi-dence, concentration, manifesting, alertness, sunni-ness, happiness

When you think of the color yellow, what comes to mind? You probably think of the sun or something upbeat and happy, right? That is exactly what this color means. The sun in magical practices, and even some religions, liter-ally means life. Wearing yellow, carrying yellow crystals, or using yellow crystals in your spells and rituals can call upon happiness, joy, and abundance. If you need to inject the feeling of happiness into your life, then grab a yellow crystal like citrine and go! Your solar plexus chakra is where your manifesting powers come from. It is the third chakra, located right by your belly button. When this chakra is balanced and flowing, you will be motivated and able to take aligned actions on your desires. You will know who you are and what you want, and you will go for it!

Green

Chakra: Heart chakra

Crystals: Jade, aventurine, emerald, peridot, malachite, green calcite, amazonite, apple aura quartz

Keywords: Nature, healing, change, expanding, growth, balance, life

Next up on the chakra ladder is the heart chakra, which is represented by both green and pink. I am starting with the color green. You see green in the beauty of nature, and that is what this color is all about. This magical crystal color of the earth is grounding and healing. It is also the color of money! You probably already know that green relates to money and abundance, so having green crystals will help you call that into your life. Now you can see why the Chinese worship their jade, as it can bring prosperity and good health. Working with a green crystal can also expand your heart energy. Life, love, beauty, and compassion is what your heart chakra represents. Through this heart balance, you can find love, health, and abundance. Green is telling you to appreciate the beauty around you so that you can attract more prosperity into your life.

Pink

Chakra: Heart chakra

Crystals: Rose quartz, pink opal, cobaltoan calcite, kunzite, morganite, rhodonite

Keywords: Love, unconditional love, calm, confidence, acceptance, contentment, beauty, self-worth

On Valentine's Day most cartoon hearts are pink, so it's no surprise that pink is also related to the heart chakra! Even though green is associated with the heart chakra as well, some people visualize it as pink. Both are amazing healing colors, so whichever you prefer is fine. The color pink is associated with self-love and unconditional love. It is connected to gaining self-confidence and being able to follow your heart. When you are aligned with what you truly desire and are guided by love, positive opportunities will show up in your life and you will feel fulfilled. Pink crystals can help you be kinder to yourself and enhance all relationships because this soft, gentle color will help you understand with compassion and empathy. Pink wants you to remember that it all starts with loving who you are.

Blue

Chakra: Throat chakra

Crystals: Lapis lazuli, celestite, sapphire, kyanite, aqua
    aura quartz, turquoise

Keywords: Truth, cool, calm, soothing, peace, communi-
    cation, heavenly, celestial

When I see blue, it reminds me of the soothing ocean
or the serene, beautiful sky. This color brings a magical
energy of calmness. It is the color of trust, loyalty, and
honesty. When you want to bring a pure, peaceful energy
into a space, place a blue crystal in the center of the room.
Blue is the color of the throat chakra, which rules communication and speaking our truth. When you want
clarity in your thoughts, or when you speak, carry a blue
crystal to enhance communication. Blue crystals are perfect for speakers or singers who want to joyfully express
their true voice to others. Blue reminds you that peace is
within; sometimes you just have to dig deep to find it.

Purple/Indigo

Chakra: Third eye chakra

Crystals: Amethyst, purple fluorite, spirit quartz, amet-
    rine, lepidolite

Keywords: Psychic, intuition, protection, mental clarity,
    imagination, creativity, magic

Throughout history, purple has been associated with the energy of nobility, mystery, and magic. Working with purple can help you get in touch with your intuition, activate your psychic powers, and give a magical boost that stirs your creativity. The third eye chakra is located right in the middle of your forehead, and it can be imagined as a purple or indigo color. Sometimes I literally see an eye opening to receive the intuitive messages from the Universe. This chakra governs your imagination, awareness, and inner wisdom. Purple crystals, like amethyst, can also be used for protection when you are sleeping, to get rid of headaches, and to gain mental clarity. Let purple spark your imagination and creativity.

White/Clear

Chakra: Crown chakra

Crystals: Clear quartz, apophyllite, diamond, Herkimer diamond, selenite, moonstone, phantom quartz, angel aura quartz

Keywords: Purity, angels, higher self, master healer, truth, ascending, kindness, high vibes

White and clear color magic represents new beginnings, purity, and the feeling of being cleansed and whole. You can think of white as a blank canvas that you can work with. If you need a certain color crystal but it is not available to you, you can use white as a stand-in. Many white crystals are connected to the moon and feminine energy, like selenite and moonstone. White and clear crystals are master healer gems that can help accelerate healing energy for your mind, body, and spirit. They can also be used to cleanse and purify the energy of a space or around a person. White and clear crystals bring in new, positive vibrations. White color magic is associated with your crown chakra, which sits just above your head. Some people see the crown chakra as a white or rainbow lotus flower. This is your divine connection to spirituality and your beliefs. When the crown chakra is balanced and activated, miracles and magic appear in your life. You just have to believe.

Black

Chakra: Root chakra
Crystals: Obsidian, smoky quartz, jet, black tourmaline
Keywords: Protection, grounding, dispels negative
    energy, wisdom, manifesting

Black is like the darkness of the moon, where everything is hidden and secretive. By being hidden, black can protect you from negative energies, emotions, and chaos. It is also a grounding energy, which brings us back to the root chakra. The root chakra and black color magic are all about survival and being mindful of your physical world. Black crystals can help you ground your ideas and manifest your goals while protecting you at the same time. These magical black gems can repel fear and doubt so that you can move forward. Black tourmaline can be placed near the entryway of your home for protection. Playing in the dark isn't a bad thing, as sometimes you need to face the shadows before you can welcome in the light.

EXERCISE
Chakra Crystal Healing

Are there areas in your life that you would like to heal, such as your health, love life, finances, or anything else? As we have already discovered, the colors of the crystals also correlate to the energetic centers of our bodies known as chakras, which govern spiritual, emotional, and physical health. If there are any issues popping up in your life, it could be that the flow of energies in your chakras are blocked. Using crystals as a healing tool for your chakras is ideal and powerful.

For this exercise, first pick an area of your life that you want to heal, then choose the crystal that can help you with your challenges. With the crystal that you have chosen, see which chakra it is related to via color magic. Use figure 1, which shows you where your chakras are located on your body, and place the crystal on its corresponding chakra. Close your eyes and imagine a healing light traveling from the crystal into that chakra, clearing and unblocking anything that is not needed there.

This exercise can be done for however long you want, but I would suggest starting out for three to five minutes, then moving it up to fifteen to thirty minutes of healing. This exercise can be used daily or whenever you are in need of a little boost of positive vibes.

Crystal Tip
Size Matters

Many of my clients ask me, "Does size matter?" The answer is yes, in some instances. If you are carrying a crystal with you or keeping one on your bed or desk for personal use, any sized crystal is fine. If you are calling good vibes into a room, you might want to get a larger crystal for the room, or you could put a few smaller ones around the room, depending on their size.

While there is no exact measurement for how big of a crystal you need for your healing or situation, I believe that crystals emit light, and the bigger the crystal, the more light and energy it will have. However, trust your gut feeling. If you want another crystal in the living room by your unicorn statue, then put one there!

Chapter 4
Your Magical Crystal Collection

Whether you are a first-time crystal collector or a crystal lover, I am super excited to help you cultivate a magical, high-vibe crystal collection that is fully aligned with what is best for you! In this chapter, I will be sharing my knowledge on how to take care of crystals and how to work with them, magically and non-magically.

The sparkly information I am sharing is based on questions I have gotten from my crystal clients. Many were curious newbies or first-time crystal collectors, and they had so many of the same questions.

On a side note, working with your crystals should be intuitive, based on what feels right to you. Take what resonates with you from the teachings of this book, but remember that whatever calls to you is the right thing for you.

Why Should I Start a Crystal Collection?

A huge reason why you would start your magical crystal collection is to access the crystals' powers to manifest and heal your life. In addition to the using the energies of the crystals to enhance your magical practices and healing sessions, crystals can help you ground your intentions and ideas in the physical realm, creating immediate shifts. You will see so many more ways to integrate crystals as you continue to make your way through this book.

Once you buy one gem, you will probably keep going buying more and more, especially as you continue on the path of the Crystal Enchanter. Each crystal has a different vibrational frequency that can help you achieve different goals, so by building your crystal collection, you will always have the right crystal for any situation.

How Do I Choose My Crystals?

Choosing your very own gorgeous crystals can be fun and easy! It doesn't have to be a whole significant ritual where you first connect to a deity and then channel your crystal—although you can certainly do that if it feels right for you. The most important thing when choosing a crystal is that it makes you feel happy. Keep that in mind at all times.

With that said, the easiest method of choosing crystals is to choose the prettiest one that is trying to get your attention. The gorgeous gem that you just *have* to have. You know, the one that is so beautiful you can't stop staring at it? Yup, that's the one. Your new crystal baby is winking at you, asking you to take it home. It is crystal love at first sight.

Another super easy way to select your crystal is by first knowing what you want to use the crystal for or what energy you want to call in. You can use the color magic guide from chapter 3 to help you decide. Pick a crystal that is related to the energy you want to call in, enhance, or work with, like love, money, intuition, or health. Remember that crystals choose you as much as you choose them. If the color of your crystal and the energy that you decided to work with don't seem to match, maybe it is a sign that you need to shift your focus. Let the magic of the crystals guide you.

You will naturally be attracted to the gem that matches your vibration and what you need in your life. Sometimes a crystal keeps catching your eye, but it was not the one you were consciously looking to buy when you started searching. In that case, this crystal might be calling to you or sending you a message. Most of the time, you will probably end up adopting the crystal that calls to you and taking it home.

If you are still confused or indecisive (or maybe you are a lazy Crystal Enchanter like me), let's simplify the process. Just pick an energy you'd like to work with, find where that magical energy is represented in chapters 5 through 10, and select one of the crystals that chapter suggests. Boom! Now you have a magical stone to help you manifest your goal.

Something else that is important to know is that it does not matter where you buy your crystals. You do not need to go on a long journey into the mountains or to some particular shop to purchase your crystals. You can buy from a local store or even on social media. I would suggest purchasing from a store (whether in person or online) that is reputable and that you have good feelings about. If you walk into a metaphysical store and you suddenly feel uneasy or yucky, get out of there; don't even buy a crystal. There are tons of crystal sellers, especially small business owners, that have high-vibe crystals waiting for you.

Crystal Tip
Selecting with Shapes

The way crystals are shaped or naturally formed also has different magical meanings. To choose the perfect crystal for your ritual or spell, you can pair up the meaning of the color magic and the shape of the crystal to put a laser focus on your intention.

For example, the standing quartz point, or what I refer to as a tower, is flat on the bottom and has a sharp point at the other end. This crystal works well in the middle of crystal grids (which you will learn about in chapter 11) and is perfect for calling in the magic and energy that you desire.

If a crystal has pointed ends on both sides, you can use it to call in and to send out energy and magic. Spheres are powerful energy emitters and are pleasant to have in your living room, bedroom, or any healing space. Raw clusters have many little points in one crystal. Place large clusters in areas where people gather to improve harmony and communication. If you have a two-point cluster, these crystals work well for love and relationships. Because different crystal shapes have different meanings, I buy the same type of crystal in many shapes and sizes so I can select the perfect one depending on what I'm using it for.

EXERCISE
Gift of Magic

There are rumors that a crystal's magic only works well if it was gifted to you, which is not true (although it is fabulous when someone gifts you a crystal). In this crystal exercise, you will be gifting someone a gem to brighten their day, share good vibes, share energy, and maybe even introduce your friends and family to crystal magic.

To start, choose a crystal that you feel would match the person you are gifting it to. See if that crystal's energy is one that they need in their lives. You could choose a crystal based off its energy, color, or shape—or maybe the crystal keeps winking at you. If you walk by a specific crystal in a shop or at home and keep glancing at it, or if you are scrolling online and one just seems to sparkle more, that crystal is most likely "the one." Gift this crystal and tell the recipient the meaning of the crystal (if you know what it means) or that you want to give them the crystal for good luck.

If you choose to, you can even gift a stranger with a crystal and check out their reaction. Sometimes when I am leaving the house, a gem will wink at me, asking to come along for an adventure. When this happens, I know that I will be gifting this crystal to someone. During the day, I will meet a stranger that catches my eye and then I know that the crystal is for them. I approach the stranger and kindly ask if they would like a crystal. Then I share the crystal's magical meanings with them. Usually, the stranger is super grateful and intrigued by the magic. However, if the recipient declines the crystal, pick someone else to share it with!

Sharing a crystal with another person is a fantastic practice to connect with crystals and to see how the magical gems guide you to gift them with love and pure intentions. Gifting is also good karma. Remember, the energy you give to the world is the energy the world gives back to you.

How Do I Take Care of My Crystals?

Crystals are alive, just like pets, plants, and humans. If you own stones, you should learn how to take care of them so that they can be the sparkliest and highest vibe for you. This is a must if you choose to follow the Crystal Enchanter's practice; respect for your crystals and taking good care of these magical babies is important.

Your crystal will work best if it is kept charged or cleansed. A crystal naturally sucks up the negative ions or energies in the environment around you, and crystals can even suck negative ions or energies from you! Think of your gems as energetic purifiers for your life. Like any tool, you need to keep them functional and clean for optimal results.

The more you use a crystal, the more negative energies it will collect. If you use your crystals frequently, you should cleanse and charge them at least once a month. You should also cleanse a new gem when you bring it home for the first time. If you are working with a crystal in your spell work and it has been longer than a month, wait to cleanse the crystal, as you do not want to cleanse the energy that you have built before you are finished with the spell. Other than that, you can cleanse your crystal any time you feel called to do so, especially if you have an off feeling about it.

Magical Ways to Cleanse and Recharge Crystals

Thankfully, it is easy to charge and cleanse your crystals. Now, when I say cleanse, I do not mean washing them or bathing them with soap and water. Some people do soak their crystals in salt water, but I choose not to do so because water and salt can damage some stones. Instead, I cleanse them energetically, like magic. There are many ways to do this.

My favorite way to charge my crystals is to leave them under the full moon. The full moon is potent, and moonlight will cleanse and recharge your crystal babies, giving them a magical moon bath. You can leave them out for as long as you like, although one night is plenty. You can also renew your crystal's energies under the sun. I put them out in the early morning so the sun is not too intense. I would not recommend leaving crystals in sunlight for long, especially colored crystals, because sunlight can cause the colors to fade.

You can also perform an energetic cleansing on your crystals. If you know Reiki or any kind of energy healing modality, feel free to bathe your crystal with healing energy. If you are not familiar with any of these healing modalities, that's okay. You can still do this! Just cup your crystal in your hands, close your eyes, and imagine a pure golden light coming from your heart that surrounds the crystal with loving energy, cleansing and recharging the mineral.

Sound healing is another excellent way to cleanse and charge your stones, as the energetic healing vibrations of the sound will bring your crystal back to a good vibe. You can use a tuning fork, bell, singing bowl, or chanting to realign the energy of your gem.

Selenite crystal slabs are another way to charge and cleanse your gems. Just put your crystals on top of the selenite slab to boost their vibrational energy.

The brown rice cleansing technique is another magical method that can help draw out the negative energies that your crystals may have gathered. Fill a container or bowl with brown rice and put your crystal deep inside. I suggest letting it sit overnight, but feel free to let the crystal sit for however long you feel is right. Once you feel your crystal is cleansed, remove it from the brown rice. Immediately throw away the rice, as it holds all the negative energy that was once in your crystal.

Herbal smudge wands or spiritual sprays can also be used to cleanse your crystals. Light up a bundle (or even just a single leaf) and wave the smoke over the crystal for proper cleansing. Some people don't like working with smoke, so you could also add essential oils to purified water and lightly spray the mixture on your crystals. If you do not want to make them yourself, you can purchase cleansing sprays online or at a metaphysical store.

The best way to cleanse a crystal is whatever way resonates with you, whatever is available to you, or whatever way you love to do. Also, if you feel like cleansing your crystal in some new, different way, go ahead and do so! You don't have to always cleanse your crystals in the same way. No matter what method you choose, your crystals should feel lighter and brighter—and maybe even look more sparkly—after they are cleansed.

When your crystals are cleansed and ready to go, you can keep them on your altar or in another safe space away from the sun. You can keep them by your favorite plants, next to your bed, or in your office. You can even keep them in your bra for balanced energy every day! If you aren't sure where to put your crystals and want to select a place for each of them, walk around with them and see where they choose to go. If you feel like putting a crystal in the corner, do so. If you feel like putting one in your car, do so. Your intuition will guide you to where they should go. Most importantly, do what feels right to you, and place your crystals wherever it makes you happy.

Crystal Tip
Charging Inside

If you live someplace where you are not physically able to take crystals outside to safely charge and cleanse them, there are additional cleansing techniques inside. You can leave your crystals in your car, on the dashboard, or you can put them by a window in your home that receives sunlight or moonlight. The moon moves positions over-night, so as long as moonlight reaches your window for at least part of the night, your crystals should be good to go. You can always go outside and let the moon know that you are leaving your crystals inside to charge. Ask the moon to please cleanse the crystals for you through the window. Just make sure to give thanks.

How Do I Connect with My Crystals?

Now the fun part begins! Learning to connect to your magical gems is very important in your Crystal Enchanter journey. Establishing an energetic connection is one of the first things to do when working with crystals. Connecting to crystals and working with energies is different for each person. No one will connect in the same way.

The way you access your intuition will be the way you register a connection to the energies of the crystals. There are four main intuitive ways that you can access your crystal energy.

1. If you are a visual person and learn from reading, your primary intuitive ability could be *clairvoyance*, which means clear seeing. When connecting with a crystal, you might receive intuitive hits and messages through pictures or flashes of words in your mind's eye.

2. If you are an auditory person who loves music and learns from listening to recordings, your primary intuitive ability could be *clairaudience*, which means clear hearing. You are probably sensitive to sounds and are attuned to all the details in a song; you might naturally pick out the instrumentals in the background. Or you may just love music and know that sound really affects your energy and how you feel throughout the day. When connecting with a crystal, you might receive intuitive hits and messages by hearing words or sounds in your mind or in the physical world.

3. If you are an emotional person who cries and laughs a lot, your primary intuitive ability could be *clairsentience*, which means clear feeling. When connecting with a crystal, you might receive intuitive hits and messages through feelings, like all of a sudden you feel happy or sad. You might even receive impressions in the physical world, like your body feeling warmer or colder.

4. If you are a person that doesn't need an instructional guidebook to put things together and you just seem to know how to do stuff, your primary intuitive ability could be *claircognizance*, which means clear thinking. When connecting with a crystal, you could receive intuitive hits and messages by just knowing. You may have an aha moment, and thoughts will seem to come to you quickly. You will know without knowing how you know!

For novice Crystal Enchanters, you will eventually discover what your intuitive abilities are and how to access energy through practice and experience. It is important to know that you can access all of these intuitive skills, as we all have them. The more you work on your primary ability and strengthen that one, the more your other skills will gain power.

Don't worry if you can't figure out which primary intuitive ability you have; when you receive the messages from your crystals in any of these intuitive hits, just write it down. Focus on the "what" instead of the "how." You may feel that you are imagining things at first, like you are making stuff up in your mind. You are not! You are connecting with the crystals, and you are activating your Crystal Enchanter magic. Write down everything that comes to your mind first. Later, you can analyze it. Don't disrupt your intuitive messages by questioning if they are real or not.

After you have chosen a crystal to work with and cleansed it, it is time to program and activate your gem. This step is essential to connecting with your crystal. With any kind of magical work, you should always have a focused intention to guide the energy. Having an aligned intention that is achievable, believable, and makes you light up will help you manifest your goals faster. Your intention should be based on knowing precisely what you choose to call into your life, who you wish to be, and how you choose to feel. Take some time to put passion and positive emotion behind the intention; this will make it even more powerful. When you have your intention and your crystal ready, the magic can begin! The next step is to program your intention into the stone and to activate its energy to help you reach it.

EXERCISE
Crystal Activation

Programming your crystal and activating its energies to help you get one step closer to your intentions is simple. You don't need anything but you and the crystal, and you can do this at any time. Here are the simple steps to activate and connect to your crystal.

1. Get comfortable in a seated position with your crystal nearby.

2. Take a few breaths in and out as you rub your hands vigorously together, activating your palms.

3. When you feel heat and energy in your hands, pick up the crystal you have selected and just relax.

4. Imagine energy surrounding the crystal; it can be any color, as every crystal will emit a different color.

5. See the energy around your hands getting bigger and brighter, merging with the energy of the crystal. See them integrate. When you feel or see that they have become one, hold the crystal to your heart center and say your intention three

times. (This is also a good time to talk to the crystal if you'd like to ask it to help guide you on the best path to success.)

6. Make sure you thank your crystal and show it some love!

When you are finished with the activation, your crystal will be programmed to heal and to help you achieve your goal. Carry your crystal with you until you reach your goal or achieve whatever you are called to do.

After your wish has come true, cleanse and recharge the crystal before programming a new intention.

CONGRATULATIONS!
Cue the Sparkly Confetti...

Your mystical adventure is truly about to begin. In the next seven pages, discover the gorgeous images of the main crystals that I mentioned throughout this book. Perhaps one is already calling out to you. If you are drawn to the same crystal multiple times or the image creates a tingling in your body, then you've just been chosen! That is the magical energy that you can start working with on your enchanted crystal journey.

Crystals for
Love and Relationships

Rose Quartz

Morganite

Garnet

Crystals for
Prosperity and Money

Citrine

Pyrite

Tiger's Eye

Crystals for
Health and Well-Being

Lepidolite

Malachite

Clear Quartz

Crystals for
Intuition and Psychic Powers

Fluorite

Labradorite

Selenite

Crystals for Peace and Calm

Celestite

Larimar

Blue Calcite

Crystals for
Protection and Warding

Black Tourmaline

Amethyst

Smoky Quartz

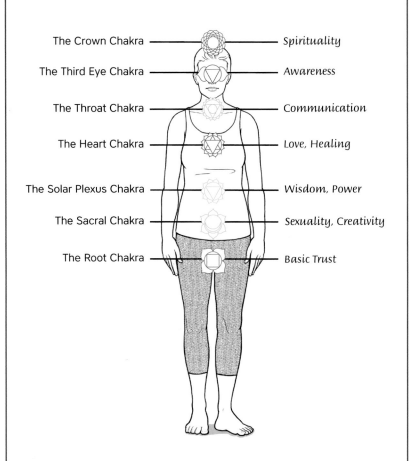

The Crown Chakra — Spirituality

The Third Eye Chakra — Awareness

The Throat Chakra — Communication

The Heart Chakra — Love, Healing

The Solar Plexus Chakra — Wisdom, Power

The Sacral Chakra — Sexuality, Creativity

The Root Chakra — Basic Trust

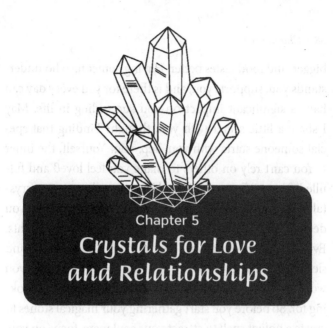

Chapter 5
Crystals for Love and Relationships

In this chapter and the following chapters in the book, I will introduce three healing crystals that you can add to your Crystal Enchanter collection. These are crystals for the six magical areas of your life, including love and relationships, prosperity and money, health and well-being, intuition and psychic powers, peace and calming, and protection and warding. For this chapter, focused on love and relationships, the three heart energy crystals you will be working with are rose quartz, morganite, and garnet.

When you are in an aligned relationship that is right for you, life seems better. The sun shines brighter, your smile is bigger, and food tastes better. Having someone who understands you, supports you, and is there for you every day can have a significant impact on you succeeding in life. May I share a little secret with you, though? Finding that special someone starts with you. Yep, you! Yourself, the inner I. You can't rely on others to make you feel loved and fulfilled. That is all you. A Crystal Enchanter knows that crystal magic is potent and can help you manifest anything you desire, but it all starts with intention and your thoughts. Even if you surround your bedroom with love crystals and sleep on them, if you don't feel like you are enough, you won't be able to attract the relationship that you are looking for. So before you start gathering your magical stones to create a potent spell to attract your soul mate, focus on you. Work on loving yourself. The good news is that crystals can help with your self-love work too.

Love and relationship challenges seem to be one of the biggest roadblocks for my crystal clients. I get more requests for love crystals than any other type. Because of past painful relationship experiences, many people have closed off the energy centers of their hearts. Their hearts are closed so they cannot be hurt again, and they will not allow themselves to cultivate another deep connection. Does this sound familiar? The crystals mentioned in this chapter—rose quartz, morganite, and garnet—emanate the energy of love and compassion. These three crystals can help you by healing your heart wounds and old traumas. Love gems can also open up the pathways of your heart so that you can be open to love. They will help you start giving and receiving love in a safe space.

Love crystals can help whether you are looking to have a fling or looking for your soul mate. If you're already in a relationship, love crystals can help if you're ready to take it to the next level or to connect deeper with your partner. Rose quartz, morganite, and garnet are easy to find and purchase, and they are full of magic. They are three of the top love crystals that I use for my Crystal Enchanter practices. I suggest them to anyone who is calling good vibes into their romantic relationships. Whether you are single and ready to mingle or in a relationship and looking to keep things interesting, it won't hurt to have a pink or green love crystal hidden in your bra or pocket, worn as a necklace, or next to your bed.

EXERCISE
Calling In Your Ideal Partner

You can use this magical exercise to help you manifest your ideal partner or soul mate. Doing this exercise will also help you gain clarity about who you choose to call into your life. The sooner you know precisely the type of person you want to be in a relationship with, the sooner you will attract them. The Universe sends you whatever you are thinking of, so be mindful of your thoughts. Be very detailed with your relationship intentions to manifest exactly who you want!

1. First, make a list of all the qualities that you want your new partner to have. You could put something on the list like "Has a lot of money" or "Has time for me." Fair warning, I've noticed that when my clients choose to call in someone financially stable, they sometimes end up with a partner that is really into their career and making money and has no time for them. This is the perfect example of why being specific in your manifestations is super important. By the way, don't be ashamed of manifesting someone with money! When you are in a relationship and don't have to worry about money, you can focus your energy on other things, like having fun together and getting to know each other. You deserve wealth and you deserve someone who is abundant because you are a magical Crystal Enchanter!

2. Now go back and look at the list of qualities that you have selected for your ideal partner. Make a checkmark next to any of the qualities that you already have and put an X next to

the qualities that are lacking in your life. For example, if I wanted a partner who cooked but I don't cook, then I would put an X next to that quality.

3. Take note of all the qualities that you have put an X next to. Here comes the magic! Those are the things that you can choose to work on to bring you closer to manifesting your dream partner. Remember, your partner is not here to fill an empty space. Your cup must already be full to attract your aligned relationship. When you work on these qualities, you can vibrate at that energetic level and the frequency of the people who have that quality. Like attracts like, and sooner rather than later, you will find your ideal partner.

4. For maximum results, make sure you also pick out a love crystal to keep with you at all times to help you open up the channels to your heart. Carrying a love crystal will help you quickly manifest your relationship intentions. Also, make sure you continue to take aligned actions in the physical world. Perhaps you should make a list of places that you could find your ideal partner, then get out of the house and meet them!

Crystal Magic Wisdom

You cannot manifest a specific person to love you if they don't. Magic and energy just do not work like that, plus it is not right to interfere with another person's life. You can write down the qualities you like about that person, and it might end up being that person, but don't have an expectation of a particular person so you won't be disappointed. Trust that the Universe has your back and will bring along the perfect partner for you.

Now let's take a closer look at the three Crystal Enchanter love crystals that can take your magical practice to the next level. These three love and relationship crystals—rose quartz, morganite, and garnet—are commonly found in stores and are some of the easiest energies to work with during your Crystal Enchanter journey. There is usually one of the three that calls to you the most; you may want to start with that crystal. But hey, if all three crystals are loving on you, get them all!

• Rose Quartz •

Rose quartz is a gentle, gorgeous, pink crystal that is part of the quartz family. It has little pink fibers naturally embedded inside the stone. Depending on where your rose quartz was mined, the color could range from a pale blush pink to a dark, dusky pink. This crystal should be kept out of the sun so that the color does not fade. Rose quartz can be found at any crystal shop. This famous love stone comes in many shapes and sizes. You can even find rose quartz carved into the shape of a unicorn! I love having huge chunks of rose quartz around my home, using rose quartz towers for spell work, and keeping small tumbled stones of rose quartz in my bra for loving vibes.

Rose quartz shares the energy of unconditional love, restoring the trust and harmony in relationships. It can help you attract love in your relationships and lead to closer connection with others. Rose quartz connects with your heart chakra, healing traumas and letting go of emotional wounds carried there. This gem can teach you how to love yourself and how to be fulfilled, content, and compassionate, which is why many also call this the self-love stone.

Also known as the stone of beauty, this crystal was used for beauty rituals in ancient times. Recently, rose quartz gua sha beauty tools have been created that are intended to lift and sculpt faces, based on ancient Chinese medicine healing techniques. I have easily added the gua sha technique to my nightly beauty routine. Using the gua sha tool is very soothing; you glide the crystal across your face, smoothing out potential wrinkle lines and any puffiness. Let this powerful crystal magnify the love that is held within your heart and fill you with beautiful, calm, and healing energy.

A Channeled Message from the Rose Quartz Collective

"Flowers bloom, flowers droop. Reach out and gather the flowers that you love before the seasons take them away, for the love that you desire is only a picking away. The most beautiful flower that blooms is the blooming of the love in your heart."

Emotional Healing

The pink energy of the rose quartz is very healing to the heart. This gem can reduce stress, calms the mind, and releases worries. The gentle, loving energy of this crystal can nourish your soul and is excellent for when you are in a midlife crisis or encountering a traumatic event.

Rose quartz can also help you strengthen your compassion and empathy for yourself and others. The healing properties of this crystal can help you foster forgiveness, releasing resentment, anger, and jealousy from your whole being.

Wear or hold this stone to amplify the feelings of happiness and love. Being close to this crystal can also help you feel serene and heal your negative emotions and thought patterns. If you are called to work with rose quartz, you are probably being guided to confront and heal some of your emotional challenges.

Magical Uses

- Rose quartz can be used to attract love or to call in your ideal partner. It can bring love, harmony, and peace to your existing relationships and create a safe, soothing environment. This gem has been used in ceremonies for centuries. Use rose quartz for love spells or rituals.

- Heal grief from a loved one's passing (person or pet) with the rose quartz crystal. This gentle, compassionate stone will release the anger and sadness that is trapped in the heart center and bring in healing.

- Wear your rose quartz on a necklace so that it rests over the heart. This can activate your heart chakra and boost confidence and self-love. The crystal will create a powerful, loving vortex that will attract more love into your life.

Crystal Affirmation: "I Am Loved"

Recite this mantra for a couple of minutes when you wake up and before you go to bed. Place your hand on your heart as you repeat "I am loved." Let this affirmation fill you with the feeling of unconditional love and the knowledge that you are loved, you have love, you can receive love, and you can give love. Believe that love is abundant. It flows in and out of you.

Crystal Tip
Double-Sided Love

One of my clients that appeared during a crystal show in Hawaii had difficulty finding love. He was hurt by past relationships and was having trouble finding someone. He had not dated for over two years and wanted a crystal to help him find a lover. We went around the showroom to look at crystals and a double terminated rose quartz was winking at him. (A double terminated crystal means it is pointed at both ends.) He purchased the rose quartz and, when he stepped into the parking lot moments later, he was approached by two girls that asked for his number. And a few months later, I found out that he had a girl-friend!

A friend of mine heard this story and purchased a double terminated rose quartz from me. She had been lonely for months, but within minutes of having her magical stone in her bra, she got asked out and had the time of her life that night. If you are looking for instant love, I would suggest you purchase a double terminated rose quartz that winks at you!

• Morganite •

Important Crystal Note: Morganite does contain aluminum, so for safety purposes, use the indirect method from chapter 12 when creating crystal potions. It is also a good idea to keep this crystal away from the sun's rays so that the beautiful pink color on this rare crystal does not get bleached out.

If you love rose quartz, you will fall head over heels with morganite. This crystal is rose quartz magnified by a thousand. Raw morganite is a transparent soft pink, violet pink, pale salmon, or champagne color. Morganite is so powerful you can feel the loving energy just by looking at this gorgeous stone. Although morganite is a bit on the pricey side, I was called to include this crystal as one of the three suggested for love because it is so powerful. You can find smaller stones for a reasonable price, and you don't need a big one because the energy is already so potent.

Another option that is very popular right now is purchasing morganite as a wedding ring instead of a diamond. They are pretty resistant to being scratched and are safe to wear all the time. Why would you buy it for your wedding ring? Well, morganite is the crystal of divine love and emotional healing, so it is the perfect commitment stone for your loving relationship. This gentle pink stone is also connected to the heart chakra and attunes to the heart. It brings compassion and assurance. Morganite attracts an abundance of loving energy into your life and will guide you in maintaining divine love as your relationship continues to grow. The strong vibration of this stone emits beautiful, loving energy that can shift the blockages in your life and replace it with divine love. If you continue to work with this crystal for a long time, you may find yourself being drawn to or more in-depth with the angelic realm, for this crystal holds a high vibrational energy.

A Channeled Message from the Morganite Collective

"The feeling of love is what we are all searching for. Up in the mountains, below the sea, and in the clouds, where is the love that is destined for us in our lives? Where could this love be? If you are one of those that ponder this question, then you may be surprised to know that love is with you all along. Love is where it should be. Love is in your heart. To know your love, to acknowledge this love, you will then attract the love that you have been originally searching for."

Emotional Healing

Morganite can cleanse the heart of discomfort and emotional blockages, helping you to release grief, loss, shame, and guilt, opening you to unconditional love, and fulfilling emotional needs and feelings.

This crystal can reawaken love in your relationships. It allows you to accept yourself and others in the relationship by bringing understanding and a powerful love vibration to the partnership.

During or after a challenging separation, morganite can assist in easing the pain and in balancing your emotions. It can help you break free of the feelings of attachment you have toward another person who does not reciprocate the interest.

Magical Uses

- Did you know that morganite was named after J. P. Morgan, the American financier who was interested in crystals? Take a piece of morganite with you when making deals, especially at the bank. This stone promotes fairness and ensures that you will get a good deal, especially when starting up a new business.

- Using morganite during your Crystal Enchanter journey can also help you develop your intuitive powers and psychic gifts. These gems can help you connect to your spirit guides and angels. Just hold it in your hands or have it touching your body while you are attempting to connect.

- When working with the stone's magic, morganite will help you vibrate with divine feminine energies, activating your beauty and power from within. This is an excellent crystal to use during a spell or ritual when connecting to a goddess.

Crystal Affirmation: "I Am Enough"

Recite this mantra for a couple of minutes when you wake up and before you go to bed. Place your hand on your heart as you repeat "I am enough." Let this affirmation fill you with the feeling of divine love. Let the energy of the crystal and these words leave you feeling strong, assured, accepted, and connected with all.

Crystal Tip
Reawaken the Love

Ready to reawaken the love in your relationship? Let the strength and magic of morganite help. Do this with your partner when you are both calm and feeling good vibes. Sit facing each other. Hold hands with a morganite in between your hands. Hold a conscious conversation with one another about your relationship. Ask, "How can we meet in the middle?" Take turns sharing. For example, you might start by sharing, "I would love for you to spend more time with me on a daily basis to help our relationship grow." Allow your partner to reply to your desires and if they can provide what you are asking for or how they can support you if not. Your partner might answer, "I agree with you, but I am very busy at work. What if we schedule a couple times a week for a special date? Would that feel good for you?" As you both listen and reply with an open mind and open heart, work on how you can compromise on this situation. Then switch roles and see how you can support your partner.

When you both have come to an agreement on how you can support each other in the most loving way, plan a new adventure or maybe a date night that fulfills both of you. Share how you can spend more quality time together. The morganite will ensure a safe container for such an important and emotional talk and allow both of you to be freed of jealousy, anger, and past negative emotions. Speak from your heart, speak the truth, and don't hold back about what you truly desire. Your partner will follow your lead and may even be surprised at what you are sharing. That can inspire them to show you what they desire as well. Most importantly, remember to take the actions that you have agreed upon. Get out there and do it!

• Garnet •

Important Crystal Note: Garnet does contain aluminum, so for safety purposes, use the indirect method from chapter 12 when creating a crystal potion or anything that is being ingested. Aluminum is safe to handle and fine for contact with your skin, but it should not be taken inside the body.

The garnet's raw shape and different shades of red always remind me of a beating heart. Like a beating heart, garnet has a regenerative and energizing healing frequency that can help inspire love and devotion. Even though garnets are seen as many deep shades of red, this crystal can appear in almost any color except for blue. Maybe the red color of this gem also reminds you of the yummy seeds inside of a pomegranate; it sure does for me.

The bold red resonates with the heart chakra, but also with the root chakra, as it will strengthen your belief in who you are and keep you grounded. Increasing your sex drive is one of its main magical energies. If you need a boost in your love life, be sure to add a garnet to your Crystal Enchanter collection.

Not only is garnet for love and relationships, but it is also known as the stone for attracting success to your business. This stone will boost your physical productivity and help you feel like you can accomplish anything in the world. In ancient times, garnets were worn on the battlefield as jewelry and incorporated into weapons and clothing. Sometimes a relationship can feel like a battle. Garnet can help you enhance the truth in your relationships, stand up for yourself, and spark passion in your life. Let your garnet assist with shifting old behaviors and opening your heart to new possibilities.

A Channeled Message from the Garnet Collective

"Seek what you know, seek what you hear, seek what you love, for seeking is the ultimate magic within you—and sometimes you don't realize that until it is too late. Everything is a cycle. You may love, you may lose love, and you may love again. Your present will not be forever. Have hope and focus on living your best experiences. Focus on loving the life that you are living."

Emotional Healing

The energy of this stone can bring on an empowering feeling, enhance your confidence to remain strong, and can lessen emotional disharmony in your life.

This powerful crystal can also ward off the emotional feelings of depression and hopelessness by infusing you with courage to deal with the situation at hand with a positive attitude. Garnet can turn negative energies into positive energies, calming the crisis and making it into a manageable experience.

A potent heart chakra crystal to help people who have suffered a loss and are still in mourning, the garnet can help lessen emotional pain and grief, providing encouragement to move forward in life with an open heart.

Magical Uses

- In spells and rituals, working with a garnet alongside your other crystals can help amplify their energies and effects, supercharging your intentions and helping you manifest them faster.

- You can jump-start your libido and sex drive with this love stone. It is also a powerful fertility stone that you can add to your rituals and spells. Specifically, I suggest placing eight garnets under your bed in a shape of a circle if you are looking to create a baby with your partner. Leave your garnet circle there for the night of the baby making.

- Keep a garnet close by when you are out and about. This protective stone can repel negative energies, keeping unfavorable people from approaching you. My mentor and friend, Leeza, wears her pendant when she is out in public, and she says it works like a charm.

Crystal Affirmation: "I Am Worthy"

Recite this mantra for a couple of minutes when you wake up and before you go to bed. Place your hand on your heart as you repeat "I am worthy." Let this affirmation fill you with the feeling of love and strength. Let the energy of the crystal and these words vibrate within you throughout your day, bringing you courage and hope.

Crystal Tip
Garnet Dreams

This protective crystal will guard you against nightmares. And if you sleep with garnet by your bed, this crystal can help you divine in your dreams. You can use this technique to unravel the mysteries of your life, including the challenges you have been unable to solve or the questions that keep you awake at night. Instead of lying awake because your mind is spinning, let the magical energies of the garnet help you find the solutions and answers to your questions while you sleep.

To divine with your garnet is very simple. Just write down your question on a small piece of paper and put the paper and garnet under your pillow before you go to bed. To extend it further, before you fall asleep, assure yourself and create an intention that you will remember your dream and receive the answer to your situation. Keep a pen and paper or your dream journal close to your bed so that when you wake up, you can immediately write down your dream—and I do mean immediately! Even if you wake up in the middle of the night to go to the bathroom, write down any thoughts that you remember. Sometimes you might not remember the dreams, and that is okay. As you go through the day, if it is important enough, your dream will come back to you. If you can't write or type fast enough, another quick way of recording your dream is to have your phone by you and record your dream as you say it out loud. Record whatever you think of first, and don't try to analyze it or make sense of your dream; you can do that later.

After you have your dream recorded or written down, go back and see if anything important stands out and circle it. See what that person, place, thing, or phrase means to you. Don't google it or look it up in a dream dictionary—see what it means to *you*. This is your dream and your subconscious talking to you, so you will know yourself best. For example, ice cream might mean different things to different people. To me, ice cream means celebration because I always eat it at birthday parties, but for someone who accidentally spilled an entire ice cream cone on themselves on a first date, it might mean humiliation. Get the point? After you have looked at your notes and deciphered what they mean for you, feel free to go back and put it all together. Be your personal dream detective. Grab your garnet for this, and remember to ask for clarity. You will begin to see patterns forming as your dreams speak to you.

EXERCISE
Love Amplification

You can do this exercise every day to amplify your connection with love and your crystals. It can be as long or as short as you want. During your Crystal Enchanter self-care magic time, grab one of your love and relationship crystals and your journal.

1. Hold on to your crystal with your nondominant hand (the one you do not use for writing) and take a few deep breaths.

2. Feel an energetic cord from the base of your spine to the top of your head, aligning your energy and your body. Then begin pulling the cord up and out of your body and into the sky. Feel the energy shoot up into the sky, the galaxy, and the Universe. This plugs you into the divine frequency so that you are open to receiving inspiration, love, and healing from your crystal.

3. Focus on the energy of your crystal and ask, "What part of my life do I need to love more today?" Start writing down whatever you think of, letting your crystal guide you. Don't worry about if it makes sense. Write as much or as little as you would like. You can also draw or doodle if you feel called to do that. When you're finished, consider the messages you've received.

4. You can also incorporate tarot cards into this exercise. Simply pull a card after asking your question and journal about that card. Write whatever comes to mind. See if you notice some sort of pattern or if the card relates to what happened during your day.

With this exercise, you can give love to the parts of your life that are lacking, creating a balanced, loving energy that will be amplified and magnified to attract others with the same good vibes.

Crystal Love Spell

This crystal love spell is to meant to attract a new lover into your life. Whether this love is a fling or your soul mate is totally up to you. Start by creating a love intention that is perfect for you at this moment, one that most aligns with what you want to manifest.

Magical Tools

Pink candle

Love crystal

Ball of pink yarn

1. Create your intention and set up your sacred space. For your intention, write down a list of qualities that you would like your future lover to have. You cannot manifest a specific person, but you can add the qualities of a person that you most desire.

2. Tune in by closing your eyes and focusing on your breath, breathing evenly and deeply with each inhale and exhale.

3. Light your candle and look into the flames. See the loving pink energy float into your body from the light of the fire.

4. When you feel like you are filled with the loving energy from the flame, pick up your love crystal and your pink yarn ball.

5. As you imagine your ideal lover, wrap your yarn once around the love crystal. Make sure you leave an extra yarn tip to tie at the end. Each time you list one of the qualities that your ideal lover embodies, make another loop around the love crystal. When you are finished listing the qualities and are able to see your lover manifest in your mind's eye, cut the string of yarn off of the ball. Tuck the yarn's ends or tie the yarn onto the crystal.

6. Now hold your magical lover yarn crystal to your heart and repeat the incantation "I am loved, I am loved, I am loved and so it is."

7. Thank the Universe, your guides, and the crystals as you tune out and bring yourself back to the present moment and into the room.

8. Let your candle burn all the way through to complete your spell. Make sure you do not leave the candle unattended if it is still burning; put out the flame before leaving the space.

9. Keep your lover yarn crystal on your altar, next to your bed, or under your pillow until your lover manifests.

Do action research as to where your particular lover would go relating to the qualities that you desire. Then actually go out to places where you could find your aligned love! For example, if one of your qualities for your ideal lover is that they are a foodie, you might find this person at a food festival or a popular restaurant. Stay open to any possibilities coming your way. Be willing to go with the flow.

———

Having the feeling of love surround you as you practice your crystal magic is very important. Love is a high vibrational energy that can heal and attract abundance. When you can love yourself and can give love to others, this is when you will feel the most fulfilled. Magic will happen, and you will be aware of the beauty that appears every day. If you infuse your spells and wishes with unconditional and divine love, you will receive back ten times what you had intended. Love is a potent magical energy that can be accessed by anyone, and now you know how to access it for yourself and your life.

Chapter 6
Crystals for Prosperity and Money

Money, money, money! Let's talk about money! In this chapter, you will discover the energies and gifts of three potent money crystals: citrine, pyrite, and tiger's eye. You can learn how to work with these abundant crystals and incorporate them into your everyday Crystal Enchanter practice. When using money crystals in your spells and rituals, they can amplify your intention and help you connect to prosperity and increase its frequency.

Like love and romance, I have had many clients struggle to bring wealth and prosperity into their lives. They tend to fall into two categories. In Group A, I have clients who have been able to make money, but they somehow spent it all and have no money left in their bank accounts. These clients were able to manifest wealth with ease, but they are unable to hold on to it. My Group B clients are those who haven't seemed to be able to manifest any money or abundance at all. These clients are always struggling to make ends meet and are missing the abundant opportunities that come into their lives. It doesn't matter what category they fall into; when my clients started working on their relationship with money and cultivating a positive mindset through the help of these prosperity crystals, changes began to happen. Money started showing up randomly in their bank account or other things happened, like their spouse getting a raise. Many have gotten out of debt. The crystals helped my clients heal their beliefs and emotions around money, and that led to being open to all the abundant possibilities that were already accessible for them.

Being abundant is not just about having a lot of money, it's about being wealthy in all parts of your life. Don't get me wrong though, money does makes everything a lot easier, so I can see why everyone asks for a money-making crystal! As a Crystal Enchanter, your magical goal is to have an excellent relationship with money so that you can consistently manifest wealth into your life. Crystals can help you raise your vibrational money frequency and help you attract prosperity into your life. Taking aligned action, like finding a new job, reaching out to new clients, and working on your mindset, will help your manifestation a lot more. The three prosperity crystals—citrine, pyrite, and tiger's eye—will be easy for you to find and purchase. These crystals have proven to bring in lots of money for myself and my clients. They have worked so well that one of my clients won $1.4 million in Las Vegas with his citrine tower! His wife bought him the crystal as a gift for good luck. I'm not even sure if he knew what crystal magic was or believed in it, but he thought that it was his good luck talisman, and he got fortunate. I'm not saying you will make millions, but if it could happen to him, it can happen to anyone, right? So, let's get you acquainted with the abundance crystals and see if you would like to add them to your crystal collection. Let's love money and love money crystals. Think about it this way: more money, more crystals!

Manifesting money comes down to your belief in it. You either believe it is a constant flow into your life and is always there to support you, or you believe more in scarcity and that there is not enough money to go around. I would invite you to take a closer look at where you are in your relationship with money before you start manifesting with prosperity crystals. Brew some enchanting tea or coffee, plop down in a comfortable spot, and unpack your money beliefs through some journaling activities.

Say out loud, "I love money." How did that statement feel to you? Were you 100 percent in alignment, or was it like, "Yeah, that's not happening for me?" Take a moment to see how it feels to you. Maybe you are somewhere in between. Whatever you feel, it is the perfect place for you right now, and as you work with the money crystals, you will see your abundance expand. If you'd like to, I invite you to look deeper at your money beliefs by journaling about the following questions:

- What is your relationship with money?
- How do you feel about money?
- Does talking about money bring up uncomfortable emotions or thoughts? Why?

Acknowledging what your actual beliefs are is the first step. When you see your thoughts on paper, they become real, and now you can do something about them! (Like the Money Forgiveness exercise in this section.) After the acknowledgment, shift and alchemize your thoughts and feelings to something that will help you get closer to your goals. It is okay to discover beliefs that you didn't even know you subscribed to in your subconscious. That is why we are working on clearing these negative blockages through the Crystal Enchanter practice.

EXERCISE
Money Forgiveness

Money forgiveness will help you tune in to the loving energy of money. Instead of feeling guilty, mad, frustrated, or sad about experiences attached to money, you will transform these energies into something positive. When you view money as loving and happy, more will flow your way. This is a simple incantation that clears negative thoughts, beliefs, and energy from past experiences. It is one of my favorite tools to use to forgive and create love for my money. You can do this exercise anywhere, anytime.

Just for this exercise, I would like for you to write down the earliest five to ten negative experiences that you have encountered with money. One memory could be when you were five years old and you heard your parents say money is the root of all evil, or when you were ten and someone stole your lunch money. Whatever comes up, write it down.

When you are finished, go back to the first experience and relive it in your mind. Imagine yourself there at the moment, feeling those negative feelings. Then say, "Thank you money. I love you money," three times. Repeat this process for the rest of your list. You should feel lighter or have some kind of release as you move down the list, letting go and forgiving the negative energies around money

experiences and bringing in the energy of love and gratitude. This money recoding exercise will help you start
building a loving, appreciative relationship with money
so that you can create an abundant path for money to
flow in and out of your life.

• *Citrine* •

I am leading off the abundance stones with citrine because
this was the first money crystal that was given to me, and
it made me truly believe in the power of crystal magic.
With the help of the citrine, I was able to manifest five
hundred dollars for a trip I wanted to take. I would say
this is when I began my Crystal Enchanter journey. One
of my most powerful crystal experiences was when I laid
my eyes on a display of natural citrine for the first time. I
was in awe, not only because of how beautiful and powerful it was, but because of how expensively priced they
were. The owner of the crystal shop said "It takes money
to make money" when my jaw dropped at how much a
huge citrine tower cost. He then told me a story about
how he won tons of money gambling after using a citrine
in his money spell.

Natural citrine is usually a pale yellow, lemonade yellow, or a deeper, honey brown yellow. Commercial citrine,
aka fake citrine, is deep orange, yellow, or brown. Fake
citrine is really amethyst or smoky quartz that has been

heat treated to get that color. I have had success working with both types of citrine crystals, real and fake, but I like the vibrational energy of real citrine better.

Citrine is known for both attracting prosperity and helping you maintain it. This good fortune stone is the number one stone for me when I am looking to manifest wealth and money. This crystal also does not retain negative energy, so because it is full of sunshine and joyful vibrations, you never have to cleanse it. Some citrine towers also have sparkly inclusions inside where you can catch rainbows. When I citrine shop for our crystal boutique, I try to find the ones with rainbows because they seem to have higher vibrational energies.

A Channeled Message from the Citrine Collective

"In the world of the citrine, we only speak joy and happiness because when you have it all, that is the vibration you are in. We do not understand the energy of lack or need. You should take those words out of your vocabulary too. Focus on what makes you happy, then get it. Get some sun, get some light, and smile."

Emotional Healing

Citrine is the sunshine stone. It is filled with positive, uplifting vibes. If you feel depressed or sad, this sparkling crystal can uplift your mood and bring in good vibes. Looking at one always makes me smile.

If you are feeling nervous or anxious, citrine can help you overcome those feelings. Citrine can help boost your self-esteem and self-confidence, giving you the courage to take action and taking you one step closer to your goals.

When you feel lazy and unmotivated, grab citrine. This gem governs action and motivation, much like the yellow color of the solar plexus, and it can help you get off your butt and take action.

Magical Uses

- Put a citrine crystal in your wallet, checkbook, or cash box to attract money and abundance into your life. Citrine is also known as the merchant's stone and will help you manifest financial success.

- Wear a citrine studded crown to promote creativity. Your gorgeous crown will also enhance concentration and bring mental clarity. As a matter of fact, I'm wearing one right now.

- Create citrine elixirs to spray around the room to dispel negative energy. Fill a spray bottle with wild orange and lemon essential oils for an uplifting smell and to call in positive energy. You can read more about crystal potion sprays in chapter 12.

Crystal Affirmation: "I Love You, Divine Money"

This is a very powerful mantra because money is energy, and energy is what flows all around us and is connected to everything in our lives. Learning to love money and the energy of abundance is very important. When you love money, you will be able to manifest your desires. Recite this affirmation for at least two minutes daily—and whenever you think of it. You could even set a reminder on your phone to say it every hour. Embed this magical energy into your mind, body, and soul.

Crystal Tip
Attracting Electronic Money

This magical technique works well for those of you who earn money through your phone or computer. If you get paid over the internet, you can do this now. I was just starting my business when my BFF gifted me with a citrine tower. It was love at first sight. I carried it everywhere with me and always had it on my desk when I worked. One night I thought, *What if I put my citrine on top of my computer to attract wealth?* because that was the main item that I was using to make money in my business. I thought that since putting citrine in a wallet works, why wouldn't it work on my computer? I did just that and the next day, I kid you not, ten new clients had messaged me for a reading. At first I was thinking, *Where did all these new clients come from?!* Then it hit me—*Aha! It was the citrine magic!*

I also shared this with my soul sisters and roommates at a business retreat that I attended. When my friend Kelsey got home, she put her citrine on her phone and boom, someone messaged her to sign up for her program and was begging to get in! Kelsey contacted the potential client and she signed up on the same day. Of course, Kelsey shared this with our magical group and our friend Amanda decided to do it as well. She also put citrine on her phone overnight, and the next day, *cha-ching*! Amanda woke up to $1,888 in her account. Even if you don't believe it, it doesn't hurt to try this simple Crystal Enchanter money magic with your citrine. Just make sure that you are using a citrine tower!

• Pyrite •

Important Crystal Note: When working with this crystal in your potions, use the indirect method from chapter 12 to avoid creating brews tainted by sulfur or moldy pyrite crystals. Pyrite is not toxic to handle on skin, but if you leave it directly on your body for too long, it can turn your skin a green color.

Fool's gold is a popular name for this little gem because it's often mistaken as gold by untrained eyes. Pyrite grows in a cluster, like a lump of gold, and it has that golden yellow metallic color. The name comes from the Greek word *pyros*, meaning fire, because when this crystal is struck together or on a hard surface, you can create sparks like fire. Although this crystal cannot bring you the amount of money that gold can when sold, this abundance crystal holds the vibrational energy of financial success and wealth. This golden crystal can bring good fortune and luck to your business, especially when you are making new deals. Pyrite crystals are a bit cheaper than citrine, so if you are buying a money crystal on a budget, this would be the perfect stone for you. You will be able to find mini clusters in shops for between five and ten dollars. Many of pyrite's magical properties are exactly like citrine, and either of them would work very well for a money spell or ritual.

Pyrite is resistant to scratching and holds up well in your wallet or bag. Just don't put these crystals in your bras because they can hurt. Believe me, I've tried it! Also, your sweat and skin acid will slowly cause the crystal to alter, deteriorate, and release toxins that are not healthy for you because it is a sulfide mineral. This crystal is not suitable for creating a crystal potion or to be added directly to water you will be drinking in any way because it is toxic to our health, but you can set pyrite on your altar or crystal grid to manifest money.

A Channeled Message from the Pyrite Collective

"Some say we are gold; some say we are not. No matter what others say, we know that we rock. Our sparkly self is filled with abundance and prosperity. What you see is what you get. If others ever doubt you, let them. Let their doubts pass right by you while you continue on your golden path to acquiring your wealth."

Emotional Healing

Pyrite has light and fun crystal energy. This crystal can turn your frown upside down and inspire you to play again. When I work with pyrite magic, I always feel like I'm a kid again, bouncing around with lots of energy.

The bright gold sparkles of the pyrite can inspire you to take aligned action and to drive over your challenges like they are only a speed bump. Pyrite can infuse you with courage. You will suddenly have the drive to accomplish all your tasks.

When you feel like you are in misalignment, pyrite can shift you back into alignment. The magic of this crystal will help you see the truth of what is happening in the moment instead of making judgments based on your past experiences.

Magical Uses

- When studying, have a pyrite crystal on your desk to help enhance your memory and mental clarity. When you need to recall what you were studying, bring the pyrite out again and let this magical crystal help you find the memory that you've stored in your mind.

- To dream of your next money-making idea or action plan, put pyrite under your pillow. Before you fall asleep, make sure you affirm what it is that you want to dream of, and ask that you will remember it in the morning.

- When you are paying your bills, have your pyrite out. This shiny crystal can chase away your poverty mindset and remind you that you are abundant in every way. Paying bills will feel good and joyful. The money going out will come back to you three times over.

Crystal Affirmation: "I Am a Magnet for Wealth"

Recite this mantra for a couple of minutes when you wake up or do something work-related. Imagine a golden light coming from the Universe and showering you with sparkles. Feel the energy of the pyrite crystal. Infuse it into every cell of your body with prosperity, wealth, and abundance.

Crystal Tip
Pyrite Quartz

Pyrite and many crystals naturally grow together, but one of my favorites is pyrite and clear quartz. This magical duo forms a powerful combination that pulls you into a state where dreams instantly manifest. My favorites are round ones because they look like golden snitches from the Harry Potter movies. Pyrite quartz has the abundance and the manifesting energies of pyrite and the added amplifying power of quartz. Working together, they will support one another's magic to help you receive your wishes sooner. A high vibration and excellent quality pyrite quartz might be a bit on the pricey side, but as a Crystal Enchanter, it is worth it to add one to your money crystal collection.

Ask your pyrite quartz to attract positive opportunities into your life that will propel you to success. The energy of this unique gem will also raise your confidence and give you a boost of motivation. If you are ready to receive infinite possibilities in your life, then find the pyrite quartz that is winking at you and claim it now.

• Tiger's Eye •

Tigers are an essential part of Asian culture, and these powerful, magical, and mythical beings are in many legends and stories. When I was growing up, I was told that the tiger's eye came from these magical tigers in the myths and that this crystal would help bring prosperity and strength into my life. If you look closely at the tiger's eye, you will notice that the base color is brown and there are yellow and gold stripes running through the gem. The crystal also has a shimmering finish that glitters when you move it around, similar to a tiger's eye looking right back at you. Interestingly enough, tiger's eye crystal is also known for its powers of all-seeing and can help you sharpen your inner vision. Tiger's eye is prevalent in rings, watches, and other types of jewelry.

There are a few varieties of tiger's eye that grow naturally. Ox eye has a base color of a reddish or mahogany color. Cat's eye looks a little bit different than tiger's eye; the fibers are straight, creating a single band of reflective light across the crystal like a cat's eye. Falcon's eye, of course, looks more like a bird's eye, and it has a base that is a blue-gray-greenish color, also called blue tiger's eye.

If you are taking a financial risk, going to gamble, or on your way to buy a lottery ticket, tiger's eye seems to bring good luck and has helped my clients win. Perhaps it gave them the powers to "see" what cards the other players hold in poker or to "see" the winning lotto numbers. My suggestion is to try out different crystals until you find the one that matches your energy and can help you enhance your prosperity. Tiger's eye is an excellent money crystal to start with.

A Channeled Message from the Tiger's Eye Collective

"Hello, meow there. We are the tiger's eye collective—not real tigers, but we love kitties. Just like cats, we are sly and mysterious. Money will mysteriously appear in your life, if you decide to work with us. Make sure that you know exactly what you are calling in or we can get crafty and manifest a surprise for you. Off you go now! Call in abundance and be in the energy of money."

Emotional Healing

If you have feelings of jealousy or "comparison-itis," this crystal can help you overcome these emotions. Tiger's eye will help you feel like you are enough and will also help you understand what you truly desire.

This gem can help you be more compassionate and caring toward others and maintain ethical boundaries. Its energy will bring awareness to the feelings and desires of the other person so that you can decide how to help them best, making this an excellent crystal for understanding the needs of yourself and others.

For those who have low self-worth and an inner dialog full of self-doubt, tiger's eye can provide support in letting go of those low-vibe feelings, ensuring that change can be positive and guiding you a step closer to your goals.

Magical Uses

- You can use a tiger's eye to honor the Egyptian goddess Sekhmet for rituals and spells. Sekhmet, usually depicted with the head of a lion and the body of woman, is the goddess of war and healing. In Las Vegas, where I live, we have a goddess temple mostly dedicated to Sekhmet. When I visit the temple, I offer a tiger's eye as an exchange for helping me reach my goals.

- Tiger's eye is a trendy stone to be used as an amulet or talisman to ward against negative energies and bad luck. Tiger's eye talismans will bring you good fortune and success.

- The powerful shining energy of tiger's eye can help you focus on what your true essence and passions are, creating a motivating drive for success. With the support of this fantastic crystal, you will be able to overcome any blocks and attract abundance.

Crystal Affirmation: "I Am Money"

Say your money affirmation for a couple of minutes daily. When you are saying this affirmation, imagine yourself connecting and being fully integrated with the energy of money. Envision yourself covered in a golden light that has many cords shooting out into the world, connecting with money that will flow into you. You are money, and money is you.

Crystal Tip
Tiger's Eye with a Money Tree

Did you know that you can grow your own money tree at home? *Pachira aquatica* is a tropical wetland tree that grows in the swamps of Central and South America. This tree is also known as the money tree or the good luck tree. This plant is very popular to use when calling good energy into a space. It is even used in the prosperity corner of Feng Shui.

The money tree is a very easy indoor plant to take care of, and it is tough to kill. When I bought my second money tree for my office, my tiger's eye begged me to put him in the plant. I usually put an amethyst (or another random, water-safe crystal that chooses to be with the plant) in the soil of a new plant. This was the first time I had tried a tiger's eye.

I stuck a small tumbled tiger's eye in the soil of my new money tree and asked for them to take care of each other and bring some money to my business. Guess what? The next day I received two random sign-ups for the course that I was launching! I was not actively promoting it yet, so these sign-ups were a huge surprise. Thank you, money tree and tiger's eye!

If you add crystals to your plants, you might occasionally feel the need to move the crystal. If you do, that is the crystal speaking to you, letting you know that they are ready to be somewhere else. Other than that, you can just leave the crystal in the pot and forget about it. But don't forget to thank your crystals and plants for helping you call in abundance!

EXERCISE
Money Ritual

It is essential to be aware of the money that is flowing in and out of your life. Money is energy, and money is alive. To be in abundance and to call in prosperity, first you have to be aware of the energy. To focus your energy and thoughts on money in a positive way, you can do this simple exercise weekly. Make it part of your routine; make it into a habit.

Start by having a designated money crystal that you work with weekly. It can be any of the three crystals in this chapter or any crystal that resonates with the energy of money for you. Place this crystal in your wallet and select a day each week when you will be performing this ritual.

On your chosen day, open your wallet with your crystal inside of it and say the amount of money that you would like to manifest that week. For example, "I have manifested one hundred dollars of new money into my life this week, and I am grateful for this abundance." Then close up your wallet. During the week, keep a notebook or take notes on your phone about how much money is coming into your life. Even if you find a coin on the ground, pick it up and record it. This will show the Universe that you are aware and open to the flow of money coming into your life. Don't forget to say "Thank you money" every time you write down the amount that has come to you.

At the end of the week, show gratitude for every cent that came into your wallet and bank account. Then get ready for another abundant week!

Crystal Money Spell

This is a crystal money spell to attract money and abundant energy into your life. You will be learning to love money, and you will be calling in more money. For your intention, think of the amount of money that you would like to manifest during a specific time frame. Next, take a deep breath in and double that amount! Yes, that will be the amount that you will be manifesting because if you hit it, you will be super happy, and if you almost hit it, you will still be satisfied.

Magical Tools
Money crystal
Cinnamon powder
Money (choose the highest denomination bill you have)
Paper
Pen

1. Create your intention and set up your sacred space.
2. Tune in by closing your eyes and focusing on your breath, breathing evenly and deeply with each inhale and exhale.
3. Write down your intention on the piece of paper. Sprinkle it with cinnamon powder and fold it up.
4. Wrap your money around the paper and place your money crystal on top of it. Put your hand on top of your crystal or wrap your hand around your crystal, money, and paper.
5. Visualize what you will be doing once you receive this gift of money from the Universe. For example, what will you be doing with this money? How do you feel having this money?

What are you seeing, hearing, touching, tasting, and smelling in this event that you have already created?

6. When you are done, say, "I love you, money. Thank you, money." Say this, until you feel the love of the money and feel so grateful that money supports you.

7. Tune out and finish up your spell by breathing deeply and being aware of your physical body and coming back to the room. Thank the Universe, your guides, and the crystals for guiding you on this abundant path.

8. Put your money and intention in your wallet. Feel free to put it in a plastic baggie or something if you don't want cinnamon powder all over your wallet. Carry the crystal with you at all times as a money talisman. Throughout the day, feel free to say, "I love you, money" and, "Thank you, money" as many times as you want.

9. Record the money that is flowing into your life, even if it is one dollar. Keep track of all the money that you find or receive until you have reached the end of the time frame that you set

for yourself during your intention. You will see
so much abundance coming your way!

———

Being an abundant and prosperous Crystal Enchanter
is a plus because you can buy all the crystals, herbs, and
handcrafted magical tools that your sparkly heart desires.
Most importantly, money is here to serve you so that you
can help others. Can you imagine if all the billionaires in
the world were heart-centered, spiritual Crystal Enchanters? How amazing could they make the world?

Money is just an energy. It is the tool that we use for
exchange at this moment; it is not bad or good. It is up
to the person who owns and holds the money to decide
how they will use it to influence themselves and the lives
around them. When your Crystal Enchanter purse is full
and abundant, you can share and spread the magic to
whomever, however you choose. Let crystals help recode
your mindset and reprogram your energy to welcome in
the magical energy of prosperity.

Chapter 7
Crystals for Health and Well-Being

One of the most important things people tend to overlook—at least until something happens—is their health. Why is your health so important? Well, I believe that if you are sick and your health is lacking, then having money and love won't matter. In this section of the book, you will be introduced to three of my favorite healing crystals: lepidolite, malachite, and clear quartz. Although all crystals are healing and can be used for promoting good health, I find that these crystals can provide more focused energy for unbalanced health issues.

When your health is failing, you may have to take a break from work, causing you to lose money while you also have to spend money on medical bills. When your health is in shambles, relationships might become strained if you need to depend on your partner for assistance. Also, how can you go out on dates if you don't feel well? So, to me, health is an essential focus of my life. You will see that the energy of money, love, and health are connected. If you have a great relationship with your health, you can cultivate amazing relationships with the other energies too.

I did not realize how important health was in my life until 2018. Throughout my life, I've been pretty healthy. At the beginning of my spiritual Crystal Enchanter journey, I helped many of my clients treat and heal their health challenges, but truthfully, I was never able to understand their experiences and the depths of their pain until, out of nowhere, my health started failing. Many would say what a terrible experience it was, and at that time I would have agreed, because I had never felt so awful in my life. However, as I look back now, I see that sickness as something I was called to experience in order to shift to the next level of my spiritual path.

Getting sick made me dive deeper into my magical practice. I doubled down on my manifestation mindset (and of course, crystal healing). I created a daily healing ritual for myself, both to stay sane and to simply have hope that I would be healed. In my own personal experience, crystals have helped me manage pain and find emotional balance. Crystals assisted in my healing. Just so you know, I did not just pick up a crystal and immediately become healthy again—I wish it was that easy. For a year, I focused on positive mindset work, creating healing crystal potions and using all the magical Crystal Enchanter techniques that have I shared in this book. My symptoms started getting better and better, and all of a sudden, they were gone. The healing energy of the crystals helped me get through the worst year of my life, and I hope that they can help anyone else in need.

When you feel pain or experience health issues, it usually means that something in your energetic body is off-balance and it is manifesting itself physically. Often, when you heal your mind and soul, the body naturally follows. People eat right and exercise for the physical body, but when do we ever take care of our energetic body? Crystals are one of the best energetic healing tools.

Remember, belief creates results, and results fuel belief. As I said, you cannot expect to be healed instantly by a crystal, although sometimes miracles do happen. You have to have the passion, the desire, and the super-strong belief to be healed. You have to be willing to go on this healing journey and experience incremental shifts—and you have to be grateful for each shift. You have to believe that healing is happening and that you will be healed. You have to be detached from stories or past experiences that are holding you back. You have to be committed to doing the work. If you do this, you might not even need crystals; but with crystals, you can accelerate your healing even faster. Crystals can also help you tune in to your intuition, so make sure that you are open to suggestions and trust your instincts. To help you on your healing journey, I will be sharing with you the three health and well-being crystals that have worked for my clients and for myself.

EXERCISE
Healing Headaches

One of the most common health challenges I have come across is headaches. This magical exercise can help with a minor headache or a full-blown migraine. I came across this headache cure in the beginning of my Crystal Enchanter journey, and I have been using it and sharing it ever since.

You first need a tower crystal, which is a crystal that stands up because of its flat base and has one pointed tip at the top. I like to use clear quartz or amethyst for my healing, but feel free to use any healing crystal or mental clarity crystal that calls to you. Then follow these magical steps:

1. Lie down and get comfortable. This process will take twenty minutes. You can play some soothing music if you'd like; sometimes I listen to crystal singing bowl sounds as I heal.

2. Place the crystal in the middle of your forehead, where your third eye rests. Set it on its base so that it stands upright.

3. Close your eyes and set an intention to relieve your headache.

4. Visualize drawing the headache out of your head and shooting it into the Universe with love.

5. Relax and keep your eyes closed during the healing. If you fall asleep, that is perfectly fine; it might mean that your body needed the rest.

6. After twenty minutes, you can put your crystal aside. Charge it under the next full moon to cleanse.

Most times, my headache goes away immediately, but sometimes it goes away in an hour or so. If your headache does not go away, there may be deeper healing that needs to take place. You could do the crystal exercise for a longer period of time or seek out a professional healer that can shift the energies for you.

• Lepidolite •

Important Crystal Note: As I've worked with lepidolite, I have noticed that it does get crumbly. If you are creating crystal potions, the indirect method from chapter 12 is the best way to use this crystal. Lepidolite is not toxic to handle on skin, but do not leave it on your body for too long, especially if you are sweating. Do not put lepidolite in water.

The first crystal for health and well-being that I am introducing in this chapter is lepidolite. This crystal is mostly used for keeping you emotionally balanced and healthy. Feelings and emotions are powerful, and they can affect your physical health in positive or negative ways. When you are in a healthy emotional and mental state, your physical well-being will reflect the same.

Lepidolite can come in a rose pink, reddish color. The other, rarer colors of lepidolite are yellow or gray, and there is also a colorless lepidolite. They are found in Brazil, the western United States, China, and many other locations around the world. The popular metallic, rosy lilac lepidolite (a form of lithium mica mineral) can only be found in Zimbabwe.

When my clients are stressed or require emotional healing, the first crystal I suggest is lepidolite. To me, it has a soft majestic energy that won't shock your system as it heals your emotions and calms you down. The best way to use a lepidolite crystal is to put it somewhere close to you so you can feel the energy. Because of the lithium in the crystal, you should not put it on your skin for too long, especially if you are sweating. Never leave lepidolite in water; the crystal will crumble and come apart if soaked for a long period of time.

My favorite magical quality about lepidolite is the healing energy of this crystal for emotional well-being. It is one of the top crystals in my Crystal Enchanter magical toolbox to help relieve stress and feelings of overwhelm.

A Channeled Message from the Lepidolite Collective

"We come in threes; three to heal your mind, body, and spirit. Healing is a form of love and compassion. When you love and feel your best, then you are healed. The healing journey may be extended or short—depends on the person being healed—but that is all it is, a quest to discover more about yourself and others. There is no final destination, because you are always going to be healing and loving."

Emotional Healing

Lepidolite can help you through life changes and transitions by keeping you levelheaded and calm so that you will make the best decisions for yourself.

If you are stressed, anxious, or depressed, this healing crystal can help you lessen the intensity of those feelings and focus on being more emotionally balanced and loving. Lepidolite can help you experience a greater sense of overall well-being.

For those of you that are insomniacs or can't seem to sleep well, lepidolite promotes a good night's rest by calming the chatter in your mind. Place it underneath your pillow or next to your bed.

Magical Uses

- Lepidolite can help you make swift positive decisions for your highest good, helping you to understand all aspects of a situation.

- Holding space during a shamanic or spiritual journey with lepidolite magic around you will help enhance the experience for all participants. This crystal can also support the connection to the Akashic records.

- Lepidolite is the stone of rebirth. Use this crystal to support your past life journeys and regressions. As you connect to your past life using lepidolite, it can help you stay detached from the challenges that have happened so that you can experience the wisdom from those challenges instead of the energy of the trauma.

Crystal Affirmation: "I Am Healthy and Well in Every Way"

Recite this crystal affirmation for a couple of minutes in the morning when you wake up and before you go to bed. Close your eyes and, as you say this positive affirmation, feel green healing energy covering you from head to toe, enclosing you in a bubble that is healing everything and anything for your highest good. There is no need to focus on one specific thing that you want healed; the energy will know where to go intuitively, so just relax and be healed.

Crystal Tip
Lepidolite Heals Electronics

As I am typing this, I have one lepidolite in my lap, and there are two sitting on the computer. Lepidolite has been known to heal electromagnetic pollution. I learned this on my most recent crystal buying trip from one of the crystal dealers at the Tucson gem show. He also told me that this crystal can heal your electronic devices, keeping them healthy and functional. So hey, I gave it a go.

Whenever I'm a little too excited, like when I'm launching a course or doing a unique recording, my computer usually freaks out and stops working. Either my computer freezes and I see that little spinning beach ball of death or I can't connect to my internet, which typically works just fine. I think the computer picks up on my high energy and the connections get scrambled. So for the past month, I've been putting lepidolite on my computer and grounding before I even touch it, and I've seen a considerable change. My computer hasn't gone haywire yet (knock on wood).

The other day I was doing some sound healing online with my crystal bowl and noticed that the vibrational healing from the bowl would mute my microphone and it would stop working. So I found a cute little lepidolite, put it on my microphone, and abracadabra! It worked like a charm and I didn't have any issues after that. Maybe the power of lepidolite is how I am still able to type this on a thirteen-year-old computer. If that is not magic, I don't know what is!

• Malachite •

Important Crystal Note: Malachite is a toxic crystal that should be handled with care. When working with this crystal, make sure that it is only in its polished form. If you are brewing a crystal potion with malachite, use the indirect method from chapter 12 and make sure the crystal does not touch the water you are using.

Most people either love malachite or they don't. This mineral has a gorgeous green color and pattern that catches the eye. On the other hand, some people are creeped out and get the chills when looking at the swirly pattern. I fall into the "I love malachite" category, and that is why I have included this crystal in this book. This gem is one of the top three most potent healing crystals that I have come across. You can feel the healing energies from a distance. If you ever stumble across a malachite and don't know why you are drawn to this crystal, then it's probably a sign that you need some kind of healing. If you have no known physical or emotional health challenges, then the best place to use it is near your heart. This beautiful green crystal can heal the heart chakra and balance the energies there. Wear malachite as jewelry or meditate with it, but make sure that you have a barrier between you and the crystal so that it is not touching your skin.

Malachite usually grows with azurite or calcite crystals, and it has a high copper content, which makes this stone toxic. I would not go out and cut, hand polish, or mine it yourself—although, when you purchase malachite as a rough or polished crystal, they are safe to handle in that form. Just do not ingest malachite, breathe it in, or have it touching your skin for long periods of time. Luckily for us, malachite is very powerful, so you can access its healing energies without needing it to be directly on your skin. Not only is malachite a fantastic health and well-being healing stone, but this gem can also help you call in prosperity and wealth. Carrying malachite can assist in attracting good fortune and luck. This multi-magical gem is a great addition to your Crystal Enchanter collection.

A Channeled Message from the Malachite Collective

"Energy is continually moving, swirling, and swaying around you. When you are stagnant, your energy will also be unmoving. Non-movement will take your energy out of its natural state, unbalancing your energy and causing disruption in your physical and spiritual health. How can you keep moving? Shift, move, release, and flow with the natural cycles of the Universe."

Emotional Healing

Malachite can encourage you to have compassion and empathy for others by understanding their viewpoint and situation. This can lead to better and more harmonious relationships with others.

Speaking from the heart and sharing your emotions with others is another one of the magical abilities that malachite has. This heart chakra crystal can help you have the confidence to be seen and noticed.

You can enhance energies of peace and calm with the help of malachite. This crystal can help you balance your moods and stay emotionally detached from challenging outcomes so that you will always have a sense of contentment in all things you do.

Magical Uses

- The patterns on the malachite crystal sometimes form an eye, which is why it has been called the eye stone. It can help you unlock your seeing powers, enhancing your clairvoyance.
- To release pain or stale energy from your energetic and physical body, place your malachite on the disruptive area. Make sure to keep clothing or a piece of cloth between your skin and the crystal. Let your crystal draw out and absorb this energy. Afterward, make sure you cleanse your crystal.
- Malachite can help you focus on co-creating the reality that you most desire by helping you get clarity about what you want. Then you can find the most natural path to take to reach your goal and bring your dreams into the physical world.

Crystal Affirmation: "I Am a Powerful Healer"

I find it useful to remind myself how amazing the body is and how powerful the mind is. The mind can heal your physical and emotional self. You can heal yourself with just your intention and belief. When you are faced with health challenges, place malachite on the area of concern, making sure to keep clothing or a piece of cloth between your skin and the crystal. Then say "I am a powerful healer" for a few minutes. Imagine a sparkling green light surrounding that area and infusing it with healing energy. Chant this affirmation until you believe you are a powerful healer, because you are!

Crystal Tip
Malachite Jewelry

Because of its incredible healing qualities, you can find a lot of malachite jewelry online and in stores. However, I didn't realize how many fake malachite crystals there were out there until one of my trips to a gem show. I was trying to buy crystal beads for a bracelet. I was surprised to find some malachite beads because I know that they can be toxic if you wear them for too long or if you sweat and your skin touches the wet stone. I found that the jewelers either covered the malachite beads with wax or the beads were fake. This is why it is important to shop for only high-quality and real crystals, as fake crystals do not have the same healing attributes and vibrations as the real ones.

There are some characteristics to look for if you are trying to determine if you have an authentic malachite. First of all, real malachite should be cold to the touch when you pick it up. It is also a heavy crystal (heavier than plastic or glass), hard and dense. In real malachite, the swirly patterns on the crystal, called *banding,* are not consistent and every part is uniquely formed. Genuine malachite jewelry is also on the pricey side; it's not inexpensive. If you find a malachite that is warm when you pick it up, very lightweight, or not a vibrant green color, then you know it is fake.

You should always use your Crystal Enchanter intuition and judgment when shopping for malachite jewelry. If it feels good to you, then it's probably real. However, if you have any doubts, put the crystal back. If you are meant to connect with malachite, then this crystal will appear in your life again—and it will be a real one.

• Clear Quartz •

Clear quartz crystals are all around my house in clusters, towers, and tumbled stones. It is one of the most common crystals, and every crystal shop you go to will have some kind of clear quartz. This gem is one of the most powerful healing stones that I have come across, but is also friendly to people, and to other crystals, during use. Part of the main magic of this crystal is that it can amplify the energies of other crystals, so clear quartz is an excellent crystal to put in a crystal grid. This gem is composed of silicon and oxygen and is also known as the master healer. If you can only buy one crystal for your crystal collection, then I suggest you choose this stone. If you are in need of a crystal for a specific energy, but you do not own any crystals that embody that energy, then you can substitute clear quartz. For example, if you need rose quartz for love but you don't have any, you can program the energy of love into clear quartz. Clear quartz can be used for any type of healing, energy, spell, ritual, or ceremony. Also, clear quartz is the astrological crystal for all the signs. It is truly the all-around crystal.

There are many varieties of crystals in the quartz mineral family. Clear quartz is identified as a quartz crystal. It is sometimes cloudy and white, but it is usually colorless and transparent. It's common to find clear quartz naturally growing with other crystals. For example, clear quartz often grows with one of my favorite money crystals, pyrite, which forms pyrite quartz, introduced in chapter 5.

Make sure you have clear quartz in your Crystal Enchanter gem collection and, like all crystals, find those that are best for you. In my experience, the purest and most potent clear quartz come from Arkansas. For some reason, they are just are happier crystals and are so excited to work with me. No matter where your clear quartz is from, this crystal will serve you well, and you can find reasonably low prices everywhere.

A Channeled Message from the Clear Quartz Collective

"All living and non-living things have a vibration. Are you vibrating at the frequency you need to be to attract the health and well-being you desire in your intentions? Are you surrounding yourself with, and putting into your body, things of a high vibration? Make sure that you are consciously aware of your actions so that you can level up to the vibrational energy that you desire."

Emotional Healing

This fantastic crystal can help reprogram the mind and thoughts. If you are working on embedding a positive affirmation into your brain to promote better emotional health, then clear quartz can support your journey.

New and exciting feelings can also be enhanced with clear quartz. If you are looking to add newness into your relationship, life, or workspace, use this crystal to amplify this energy.

You can use this master healing crystal to heal any emotional unbalance and amplify loving feelings. If you pair clear quartz with another crystal that helps heal emotions, it can magnify the magic even more. Think of it as a double shot of energy.

Magical Uses

- Clear quartz has been used in magical practices since ancient times. Shamans use this gem to help activate and enhance their clairvoyance. If an intention is programmed into the crystal, it will be magnified.

- Placing clear quartz in your car can keep you, everyone in your car, and every car around you safe. I used to get into lots of car accidents and was pretty sick of it. I was told by one of my friends to do this, and ever since then, my car and I have been safe. My crystal always stays in the car, and I like to keep it on the dashboard to charge it during the full moon.

- Wearing clear quartz jewelry can assist with your personal healing. If you don't usually wear any jewelry, the easiest way to "wear" clear quartz is to stick a smooth, tumbled stone in your bra or socks.

Crystal Affirmation: "I Am Grateful for My Healing Body"

When you are thankful, no other emotions can show up. Hold your clear quartz crystal in your hand and take an inventory of your body, scanning your body from head to toe. While you are performing the scan, think of how extremely grateful for your health you are and how beautiful your body is. Repeat the affirmation "I am grateful for my healing body" as you do so. You can do this at any time. Perhaps you want to make it a daily ritual. I like to do this after I step out of the shower—clean, pure, and loving my body.

Crystal Tip
Listen to Your Crystals

All crystals are loving, living beings to me. No crystal is evil or wrong; they are just crystals and become what you infuse into them. If you work intimately with crystals and have been using them in your Crystal Enchanter practice, you might already start to be able to feel their energy and talk with them. If you aren't there yet, don't worry; in time you will be.

If you ever get a sense or thought to move a crystal, that is your crystal telling you that he or she wants to move, and they probably want to move right then. I have a few large clusters of clear quartz, and they always want to be moved. If they don't like where they are, they demand to be moved. If you decide to ignore your crystal's message, well, beware. When I don't listen to my clear quartz, I end up accidentally cutting my hands, arms, feet, or other parts of my body on them. Yes, I get cuts, as these babies are sharp. In the beginning, I didn't realize why this was happening to me, and it was only with a few crystals. Then I realized that after I moved these high maintenance pieces, they never cut me again.

So, if you are getting thoughts like *I should move this crystal*, then I suggest following through and doing it. Those are your babies speaking to you. You might not get cut like I do, as I think I just got some aggressive crystals, but they will be happier and sparklier if you listen to them. Be aware of your connections with your gems and the messages or thoughts that you are getting around them.

EXERCISE
Divining with a Crystal Ball

Back in the day, before magic and energy healing were ever introduced to me, I remember associating psychics with a crystal ball. I always thought it would be cool to use one, and I was surprised to find out that the ball was not made of crystal, but of glass. One day I decided to try divining with a crystal ball, but instead I used my clear quartz sphere. Wow, was it powerful! This potent method can be advantageous to have in your Crystal Enchanter practice. Crystal ball divining is available to anyone— yes, anyone can do it—but your skills and readings will improve with practice. Just follow these simple steps:

1. Get a crystal sphere or glass crystal ball that you connect with. Make sure it isn't too small; you need to have room to focus, so it should be a decent size.

2. Place the crystal ball in front of you, preferably on some kind of stand so that it doesn't roll away as you are trying to work with it. Beginners should dim the lights, as it is just easier to "see" and connect that way.

3. Tune in by taking long, deep breaths and centering yourself.

4. Put your hands over the crystal ball (touching it is optional) and imagine that the energy is coming out of the crystal and going into your hands and body.

5. State your intention or question, saying it out loud or in your mind.

6. Focus your eyes on the center of the ball and relax. Let your eyes relax so much that the crystal ball is unfocused and hazy, and just keep staring.

7. There should be smoke or some kind of movement forming inside of the crystal ball or in your mind's eye. Be patient and let it develop into an image. Don't force it. Keep a relaxed

gaze. The images that show up might be in the actual crystal itself or they may show up in your mind's eye. If the image shows up in your mind, it will be like when you imagine things; images or words will just pop up out of nowhere.

8. Write down everything that you "see." Don't question it, just write.

9. Tune out and take some deep breaths when you are finished, then thank your crystal ball, your guides, or whomever you were connecting with.

10. Go back and look over what you wrote. Now you can analyze it and see how it relates to your intention or question.

If you are new to divining or reading with crystals, you might not see any images at first, or they may not make sense. Keep practicing! Make a note of your progress and what you are viewing. You will eventually be able to make sense of the readings and add another magical tool to your Crystal Enchanter practice.

Crystal Health Spell

This crystal health spell is to boost your immune system. When your physical body is strong and healthy, your energetic body will be as well. Having a healthy lifestyle and body can help you stay in a high vibe and tap into your Crystal Enchanter magic with ease. Do this spell for an energy or health boost; just make sure that you are exercising, taking care of your body, and eating right also!

Magical Tools
Health crystal
Glass of drinking water
Your shower

1. Create your intention and set up your sacred space.
2. Tune in by closing your eyes and focusing on your breath, breathing evenly and deeply with each inhale and exhale.
3. Hold your health crystal in your left hand and your glass of water in your right. While you are doing this, imagine yourself feeling healthy and well in every way and full of energy. Imagine the energy of the crystal passing through your body, infusing every cell of your body with healing magic. Then see the energy go into the glass of water in your right hand.
4. Say this incantation out loud: "I invoke the healing energies of this crystal into this water. May

I be blessed to be healthy and well in every way for my highest good. And so it is. Manifest, manifest, manifest."

5. Put your crystal down and drink your water. Feel yourself become one with the healing energies of the crystal.

6. Get up and jump three times. Then turn on the shower and shower in the coldest temperature you can tolerate, massaging your body for at least one minute.

7. When you get out of the shower, grab your crystal and do a dance that celebrates your vitality, health, and magic. You can do this dance naked if you'd like, or you can put some clothes on—whatever feels best for you!

8. Shout "Yes, yes, yes" with your hands in the air.

9. Sit back down and refocus on your breath as you bring yourself back into your body and the present moment. Thank the Universe and your guides for protecting you during the spell and for helping you be healthy and well.

10. Keep the crystal on you throughout the day until you feel that the healing is complete. Grab it whenever you need some energy or a pick-me-up.

———

Health and well-being are so important. A Crystal Enchanter knows that if your cup is not full and healthy, then you will run out of magic for others and you won't be able to show up as your best self. Remember that it is essential for you to cultivate a healthy lifestyle and have balanced emotions before you can help others.

Take a look at your life at this exact moment. Are you living the best that you can be? Are you taking care of your physical, mental, and spiritual health? What are some things that you can do to feel healthy and well in every way? It all starts with your intention and then moves into action. Maybe you are thinking of exercising or eating well, but you aren't doing any of the things that will make you healthier. Know that you don't have to do anything that you don't want to do. If you don't like going to the gym but you love dancing, then do that instead. Think of creative ways to nourish your body and passion. Crystal magic can assist with reaching your goals and creating a healthy lifestyle, but you have to set intentions and take aligned actions too.

Chapter 8
Crystals for Intuition and Psychic Powers

At the beginning of my spiritual path and my Crystal Enchanter journey, I had moments where I thought to myself, *Am I crazy and talking to myself, or is this intuition?* I was receiving messages, not knowing they were from the divine and that my intuition was talking to me. Sometimes it can feel like you are talking to yourself or thinking to yourself. The messages you receive can be precise, but you might not have clarity about what to do with the message or what the heck it means. If you are at the beginning of your Crystal Enchanter practice and are currently at this phase of your learning, or if you are unable to hear or connect to the energies of the crystals, that is entirely normal. It takes time and practice to trust your intuition and to know that these messages are coming from a divine source to help you. Also, it takes time to learn how to figure out the messages you are receiving. With practice, you will be hearing and understanding messages and speaking to your sparkly gems in no time.

Three intuitive and psychic crystals—fluorite, selenite, and labradorite—are what I suggest to my clients and students when they are stuck and unable to access their intuition, or if they are having a hard time trusting their magic. In my 6 Figure Priestess Certification and Spiritual Business course, the first thing I teach the students is how to discover what their most potent, intuitive powers are out of the four clairs (shared in chapter 3) and how to strengthen them. When you are aware of what intuition feels like, it is easier to believe in it the next time it shows up. When working with these intuition and clarity crystals, they will amplify your psychic powers even more. All you have to do is be open to new possibilities, thoughts, and feelings that pop up. The most important thing about receiving messages is to trust what comes through immediately; don't question it, maybe write it down somewhere, and then analyze it later. Think of receiving intuitive hits as getting different pieces of a puzzle to solve. Some intuitive messages might be super clear, but some might be random and just confuse the heck out of you. The random ones are pieces of a larger puzzle, so do not be discouraged.

The most crucial part of receiving clear messages and tapping into your intuition is making sure that your intuitive channels and frequency are clear and unblocked. When you are not getting any messages at all, that just means that your energy and vibrational frequency is blocked and not at the highest possible energetic level for you to receive the best messages. It is very important for you to stay unblocked and to have a clear channel to receive messages from your intuition, guides, and the divine. Being blocked means that there are past experiences, thoughts, and emotions clogging up your energetic space; these could be things from childhood, like limiting beliefs or feelings.

One of the ways that you can unblock yourself is to meditate with a crystal and ask that these blocking beliefs, emotions, or thoughts be cleared and sent to the Universe with love. The more you clear and get back to your center, the more you connect with your intuition, the more you are consciously aware of what is happening in your life, the more you will grow your intuitive skill. Actually, in my certification course, I have the students practice manifesting and connecting with their intuition by asking for something fun or receiving a fun answer that can be seen, felt, or heard in real life, and they can confirm something almost immediately. It could be something small, like asking guides for a great parking spot in a busy lot, or something big, like $5,000 in your bank account. This method works especially well for my friends and me, and we use it all the time. I ask my parking angels to please find me a space, I imagine a space open for me, and it almost always works. Why is that? It's because I believe that it will work. I know that it will happen, because it's already happened before.

When you receive confirmation on your intuitive hits or manifestations, that will boost your magic even more because you will believe more and have more confidence in your skills. Having a magical Crystal Enchanter practice is just that—practicing. Never stop learning, testing out new things, being intentional with your actions, confirming your magic, or co-creating a life that you choose, and have a lot of fun doing these things every day!

Building trust with your intuition and knowing how you feel when you get intuitive hits is also key to developing your Crystal Enchanter psychic powers. Not only will these three crystals help you tune into your intuition, but they will also support mental clarity and stimulate the brain. Trust your magic, have an open mind and heart, and let the messages come through.

For those of you who have been honing in on your intuitive powers and are a pro at receiving messages, you will still find working with these crystals to be a lot of fun. You might receive messages in a new way, or your magic may be amplified even more.

EXERCISE
Crystal Witch Psychic
Development Practice

This magical practice is for newbies and advanced Crystal Enchanters alike. To this day, I practice this to keep my psychic abilities and intuition sharp. This technique is taught in my twelve-week 6 Figure Priestess Certification and Spiritual Business course for divination and psychic development, and it works. I would suggest you add this exercise to your daily rituals. It does not matter when or where you do it. As long as you keep practicing this technique, you will incrementally develop your psychic magic. The best part about this technique is that you do not need anything but yourself and a crystal.

1. First, find a place where you will not be disturbed for however long you decide you want your practice to be. I would suggest it be at least five minutes.

2. Have your crystal out and examine it thoroughly, making sure you know exactly what it looks like, feels like, and, if possible, sounds like. When you are ready, put your crystal within arm's reach.

3. Get comfortable and relax. Tuning in and getting centered, focus on your breath as you breathe in and out deeply.

4. Once you are centered, locate your third eye, which is in the center of your forehead, and imagine a sacred space there. Then clearly imagine the crystal that was just in your hands in that space in your mind's eye. Take your hands, reach for your crystal, and "pluck out" the crystal in your mind's eye so it is in your physical hands. You are now holding your crystal that was in your mind. Feel it and notice the shape, size, temperature, and appearance. Practice this for a few minutes.

5. When you are ready, poof away your mind's crystal into thin air and thank your physical crystal for working with you. Take long, deep breaths and bring your awareness back into your body, grounding yourself in the present by feeling your feet on the ground. Make

sure you are fully present and grounded before doing anything, including driving!

If you do this Crystal Enchanter psychic development practice daily, you will be more aware of the energies around you and be more open to receiving information from your intuition. If you don't have a crystal on hand, feel free to use any other object that fits in your palm. The point is not to remember every single detail, but to pay attention to how you are seeing, feeling, hearing, or smelling the object.

• Fluorite •

Important Crystal Note: Handling fluorite is perfectly safe, but like the name suggests, this crystal does contain fluorine, which is toxic if ingested. When brewing your crystal potions, be safe and use the indirect method from chapter 12.

Fluorite is one of the most beautifully colored crystals to me. This crystal comes in swirls of green, purple, clear, and blue patterns. If you hold the crystal up to the sun, you will notice a fluorescent light that highlights the different colors. During one of my crystal buying trips, I came across some gorgeous fluorite crystals from China that glowed under a blacklight. Commonly known as "the genius stone," that name describes this crystal well.

One of the leading magical properties of fluorite is that it can help support mental stimulation and enhance your concentration when studying. It is an excellent crystal to have around when you are crafting spells and enchantments for your Crystal Enchanter practice. This gem also boosts your creative energy and can help you share your gifts from the heart. My favorite fluorite crystals are in the form of towers. I love having fluorite towers on my desk as I work on my books or tarot decks. Right now, as I am typing this, I have a fluorite tower right by me, encouraging me to type with clarity. Fluorites should be very easy to find online or in metaphysical shops because it is a trendy crystal. Although there are expensive, high-quality, rare fluorites you can purchase, if you are on a crystal budget, you can find a tumbled fluorite stone for five dollars and that will be as magical as the nine-hundred-dollar piece. Expensive and rare does not mean that the stone or energy is more powerful—it just means that the crystal might have better quality and clarity or that it is rare and hard to mine. Pick out fluorite that looks beautiful and make sure it is one that you love. The stone should activate your mind and intuitive energies and help you be mentally alert.

A Channeled Message from the Fluorite Collective

"Crystals are powerful, but not as powerful as your mind. The human mind is a magical and amazing place. The power to create and grow starts from there. When you are clear with your thoughts, when you are focused, then you can manifest anything that you choose. Prepare your mind for success, and let us help you reach your goals."

Emotional Healing

This gem is a very positive, happy crystal. It is not too overly excited, but it provides a calm, soothing happiness that surrounds you when you hold it or have it near you. I like to keep fluorite in a room where a lot of people hang out so that it can help keep everyone positive.

When my clients work with fluorite, they usually report back that they seem to stop making decisions with their emotions, and they think things through with logic to make the best decision for themselves. I believe this crystal can support you in staying detached from your feelings so that you have clarity about a situation.

A flat, smooth, tumbled fluorite worry stone can help bring down your stress levels and balance all emotions. Keep one on you. When you feel a little anxious or worried, take it out and rub the stone. Tell it all your challenges, and let the fluorite absorb that energy.

Magical Uses

- If you are writing, drawing, or painting and are in a creative block, put your fluorite crystal on your working tools. Charge your tools—whether that is your computer, your paints, or a drawing book—with the magical creative energy of the stone.

- Have a fluorite crystal near you when connecting to your intuition, meditating, reading tarot, or any other kind of events working with your psychic powers. You will receive clear answers, and your intuitive abilities will be boosted.

- This gem is also great for increasing your powers of concentration and learning by helping you study. If you are memorizing tarot cards or prepping for a huge test, fluorite can boost your self-confidence and assist you in making fantastic decisions.

Crystal Affirmation: "I Trust My Intuition and Psychic Abilities"

Recite this affirmation before you go to bed. While you are repeating this affirmation, imagine your third eye, located in the middle of your forehead, as an actual eye. Imagine this eye opening up and sparkling bright. You might not see anything, but feel your magical eye opening up or shooting energy out of it. Trying this visualization as you chant your affirmation will also help you strengthen your psychic powers. If I am doing this visualization and I see crust or spiderwebs on my third eye's lashes, I know that I've been neglecting my intuition and psychic abilities for a while.

Crystal Tip
Fluorite Bath

If you are feeling stressed out, overwhelmed, and mentally drained, taking a bath with fluorite will improve your mental clarity. Having fluorite in your Crystal Enchanter magical toolbox will help you so much. When we are frustrated, things typically don't work out the way we want them to and our manifestations become blocked. To break free of negative programming in your mindset, take a bath with your favorite smooth fluorite crystal. Do not use fluorite in its raw form; I suggest using a mini tower. Make sure your crystals are clean before you use them in your bath. You can cleanse your fluorite with boiling water before you use it.

Create a magical ceremony or ritual out of this so that when you start to run your bath water, you are beginning to call in positive vibes. You can add rose petals or herbs to your bath, light some candles, and craft your bath with intention. After you have filled the bath with water at your desired temperature and added your favorite bath essentials, it's time to incorporate fluorite. You can put some tumbled fluorites into the bath to infuse the water with its crystal magic or, when you are lying in your bath, you can take a fluorite point and rest it on your forehead as you imagine your stress and frustration leaving through the crystal and being sent into the Universe with love. Of course, you can do both for double the magic. The most important part is to tell your fluorite what you want and to ask for your desires. When you get out of your magical fluorite bath, you will feel energetically and mentally refreshed, your questions will seem attainable, and your mind will be crystal clear.

• Labradorite •

Important Crystal Note: Labradorite contains aluminum and can be toxic when ingested. If you brew a crystal potion with labradorite, it is important that you use the indirect method from chapter 12. It is safe to handle labradorite on your skin.

Labradorite crystals are hidden beauties. When you walk by labradorite, you might be like, "Eh, okay, a grayish rock," but when the sun shines over the crystal at the right angle, you will see the flash and dazzle of the stone's true nature. This gem is made up of crystalline structures that are very thin and laid on top of one another in compacted layers. When light shines on the surface of this crystal it will travel down the layers, and the reflective colors we see, also known as *flash*, are mesmerizing and unique. Just like how the beautiful flashes are hidden but can be drawn out with light, labradorite can help you draw out your inner magic. Like the crystal, we have so many layers (energetically and physically) within us. Everyone is magical and everyone can be a Crystal Enchanter, but sometimes you need help to access the sparkle and the magic within. Labradorite can help you tap into your inner magic and shine for everyone to see. This crystal is super important for tapping into your intuition and psychic powers because if you know what your inner magic is and you are confident in your magic, then you will believe. Labradorite can help you understand and believe in yourself and your intuitive abilities. Labradorite can help you shift, transform, and level up. This is the stone of mystery and magic. Are you ready to uncover your mysteries and activate your magic?

A Channeled Message from the Labradorite Collective

"You are magic, and we are magic—this whole Universe is full of magic. Magic is just a form of energy that we can play with, energy to shape and form into whatever we choose for it to be. You are controlling this magic every single day with your thoughts and your intentions. Sparkle your brightest and you will see miracles appear in your life. Be amazed by the magic you hold within you, and be wowed by the magic you see in your life. Acknowledge your inner spark and be grateful for all that you have."

Emotional Healing

When you are in the presence of this crystal, you will feel calm, centered, and connected to yourself. Labradorite has very relaxing energy that can help quiet the mind and relieve stress.

If you need motivation, labradorite can help you find the enthusiasm and happiness in your task or whatever it is that you are doing. This stone can assist in developing new ideas or new ways of thinking.

Labradorite can shine its magical healing light on depression, stress, and anxiety. This crystal will help you ease feelings of sadness or anger and promote the energy of being supported and the feeling of being enough.

Magical Uses

- As I've mentioned before, this is the stone of awakening and activating your magic. Once you add labradorite to your life, you will notice that energy will start flowing your way and that what you are saying and manifesting is coming true.

- When my clients are stuck and feel like they are not connecting with their intuition or seem to have just lost their way, I always suggest labradorite as the go-to crystal. Your energy will immediately shift and your third eye will open up.

- The dazzling flash of this stone also serves a purpose. Labradorite crystals are known for their protective shielding powers. This protective power is a light so bright that only pureness and positive vibes can stay around.

Crystal Affirmation:
"I Know I Am Magical, and I Love It"

When reciting this crystal affirmation, get up and move your body. Dance, jump around, walk around, whatever you have to do to just move. Spark your inner magic with these powerful words and physical movement. I would suggest doing this for three to five minutes in the morning so that you can sparkle for the whole day. The goal is to claim this mantra and be proud of your potent magic, so scream and yell it as you dance around. Have fun with it!

Crystal Tip
Labradorite Flash

If you move these gorgeous stones a certain way in the sun, you can see them sparkling. This is *labradorescence*, which is a distinct iridescence on the gem, also known as a flash. When the stone is cut correctly at a magical angle, you can see the colors from various layers of the material that cause the flash. You can tell the quality of your crystal is good if it has gorgeous flashes. Labradorites are very magical crystals to have in your Crystal Enchanter toolbox, so next time you walk by crystals and you see a flash sparkling, stop and check them out. It might be labradorite winking at you and wanting you to take it home!

• Selenite •

Important Crystal Note: I've noticed that selenite does start to disintegrate in water and tiny pieces break off. A light spritz of crystal potion on this crystal is fine, but avoid putting this crystal in water that can cause breakage, especially if you are ingesting it. Crystal potions should be brewed using the indirect method from chapter 12 with this stone.

One of the most magically intuitive crystals that I have in my collection is selenite. I believe that this crystal has many healing powers and mystical properties. How can it not be magical when it was named after the Greek goddess of the moon, Selene? It is a white crystal that is a form of gypsum. You can find gypsum all over the world; it is the most common of all the sulfate minerals on earth. These crystals are softer, meaning they will melt and degrade in water, so be careful when working with them. Selenite is so soft that you can use your fingernails to scrape it, but I do not suggest trying this because it will cause harm to the crystal. You can find this crystal at any metaphysical shop, in person or online. Almost everyone carries selenite, and it's very affordable. Much of the selenite that you will find will be a milky white. If you see a transparent, clear selenite, that means it is of higher quality. When you work with selenite, you will be able to access higher energies and connect to higher frequencies, which will facilitate clarity with your intuitive answers. Selenite is a powerful crystal to work with for divination, and I highly suggest adding a selenite crystal wand to your Crystal Enchanter collection. A selenite wand could cleanse the energy of the room, open and close circles, tune in, and be used for healing.

A Channeled Message from the Selenite Collective

"Cleansing your energy of what is needed to be let go of is what we are here for—and to show you that when you grow and expand, things that are not in the same vibrational energy as you should be released so that you can move on. When you fully trust your intuition and let it guide you on your Crystal Enchanter path, you will notice that you are flowing with the currents of life and reaching your goals and intentions faster and faster. Things will instantly manifest, and you will feel more aligned with all your actions. Let go and flow."

Emotional Healing

Selenite is the crystal of the moon and has a deep connection with balancing the emotions. Wear or carry selenite to promote harmony, peace, and happiness.

This stone can clear away confusion, bringing on a clearer thinking mind so that you will make the decisions that are best for you without negative emotions getting in the way.

Any negative feelings, such as doubt, anger, unworthiness, or jealousy, can be cleared with the high-frequency healing of the selenite crystal.

Magical Uses

- Your magical moon crystal is a direct connection with your divine self and the angelic realm. If you are looking to work with angels and angelic healing, hold on to your selenite and tune in to your breath as you ask the divine beings to drop in and connect with you.

- Selenite can clear and open your crown chakra, giving you a boost with spiritual work. Always make sure that you are fully grounded before powering up your crown chakra so that you can root the energy into the physical realm.

- Keeping selenite near your phone or anywhere you make calls for work or business can help with communication. The energy of this crystal will help both parties speak clearly and understand all situations. It can also assist when calling a business for a refund, cancellation, or other matter.

Crystal Affirmation: "I Am Confident in My Psychic and Intuitive Abilities"

Recite this crystal affirmation when you are in the shower or the bath. Water is very healing, and it can help boost your psychic and intuitive powers. Affirming something while you are in the magical waters can help you gain confidence and access your magic faster. You can also do this every time you wash your hands or when you wash your face.

Crystal Tip
Selenite Magic

Selenite is a potent cleansing stone with pure energy. It is so powerfully cleansing, in fact, that it is one of the ways I cleanse and charge my other crystals. This methodology is preferred when charging or cleansing crystal jewelry because then you don't have to leave it outside or dunk it in any type of water. Charging and cleansing your crystal babies with selenite is so easy. All you have to do is put your crystal on top of the selenite crystal, which I find works better than laying them next to it. Selenite is a very affordable, common crystal that should be easy to find. I suggest you purchase a flat, larger selenite slab so that you can set your items on the crystal to charge. If you want to get fancy, I have found selenite charging plates that are engraved with moons and other magical symbols. You can also get a selenite bowl to put all your bra crystals in to charge at the end of the day.

Your items and objects should be touching the selenite to charge, and the more the better. If you don't want to buy a selenite slab or bowl, your selenite crystals have cleansing effects as well. If you have placed other crystals near selenite, they will be cleansed and charged slowly. Selenite itself does not need cleansing, but I like to charge it up under the full moon once in a while, just to give it some extra power. Please do not cleanse selenite in water because this will damage the crystal.

Selenite is often crafted into a lamp. This is one of my favorite lamps to own because this magical crystal can purify the air and clear negative ions. They are very beneficial to have in your rooms.

———

Learning how to connect with intuition and developing psychic abilities is so essential for a Crystal Enchanter. Everything that you do, every spell you craft, and every wish you send out will come together quickly and smoothly if you learn to trust your inner divinity and magic. Having these psychic crystals around—crystals that can instantly boost your energies and bring clarity to your magical practice—is a no brainer.

Even though these powerful gems can help you connect more deeply with your magic, it is up to you to do the work. Practice and trust your intuition and psychic abilities. Know that trust and connection can be built with time; you don't need to have a near-death experience or have something extraordinary happen to you to tap into your intuition. Everyone has it, and everyone can access it with practice.

I want to note, however, that while I am encouraging you to explore all of your magical abilities, do what makes you happiest. If something I've shared or something others have taught you doesn't resonate with you, then don't do it. Not everyone's practice is the same because we are all unique Crystal Enchanters with our own special magic to share with the world.

EXERCISE
Seeing through Your Third Eye

This exercise that I am about to share is to help you strengthen your clairvoyance, also known as seeing the physical world through your psychic eye, or your third eye. For this exercise, the main purpose is to strengthen your awareness and get you familiar with accessing the third eye.

1. Pick a room familiar to you. Take a walk around the room, making sure you see every detail of the room and the furniture. Look at every nook and cranny of the room and all the things on the shelves, tables, and other furniture.
2. When you are finished scanning the room with your physical eyes, sit in the center of the room and close your eyes.
3. Tune in by relaxing and taking nice slow breaths in and out, focusing on your breathing.
4. When you are relaxed, bring your focus to the middle of your forehead, where your third eye is located. Imagine an actual eye opening or a light coming from that location.

5. Now visualize a blank screen. This blank screen will start to fill up with the image of the room, or you can imagine yourself using your third eye to look at the room you were just in. Maybe turn your head left and right to "see" the whole room. You should be able to use your third eye to zoom in and zoom out anywhere in the room.

6. Do this for as long as you want. When you've seen all that you can, come back into your physical body. Feel your breath and the floor beneath you, and when you are ready, open your eyes.

Now, for those of you who are having trouble "seeing" the room, it is okay. That is expected for a newbie Crystal Enchanter or for those who have never worked with their third eye before. That is why I have included this exercise and practice for you. I would suggest you do this daily. Visualization is very powerful in manifestation and magic. Using visualization in your spells, rituals, and ceremony is more powerful than any other psychic sense. Also, combining visualization with emotions will double the magic. Eventually, with practice, you will be able to "see" clearly. Exercise that psychic muscle continually and you will amaze yourself!

Crystal Intuition Spell

This crystal intuition spell is to help you tap into your psychic powers, open your third eye, and confidently listen to your intuition. Instead of a massive awakening that can turn your life upside down, often this spell will help you develop your intuition incrementally. It is a great spell to cast once a month or whenever you feel like you are disconnected from your magic.

Magical Tools

Intuition crystal
Purple candle and matches or a lighter
High Priestess tarot card or image
Glass jar with lid
Paper
Pen

1. Create your intention and set up your sacred space.
2. Tune in by closing your eyes and focusing on your breath, breathing evenly and deeply with each inhale and exhale.
3. Have your High Priestess card in front of you and gaze at the card. Ask if she has any messages for you to help deepen your intuitive powers. Feel free to write whatever comes to mind in your journal, or just take note of it. Be

aware of any messages, words, sounds, smells, or even pictures that you see in your mind's eye or in the physical world. Jot them down or remember them, but try not to analyze the messages.

4. Place your intuition crystal on your third eye, in the middle of your forehead. Imagine an eye opening and shining bright or a swirl of indigo energy growing bigger and bigger. When your third eye has opened to the max, say this incantation three times: "My intuition is powerful and true; I receive clear messages to guide me on my aligned path." Infuse this incantation into your third eye.

5. Once you are powerfully connected to your intuition, write down your intention, which should be what you want to accomplish for this spell.

6. Fold up your paper and put your intuition crystal, the paper you wrote your intuition on, and the High Priestess card into the glass jar and close it by screwing on the lid.

7. Put your purple candle on the lid of the sealed jar and light the wick. Take a few deep breaths,

focusing on the flames of the candles, and seal your spell with your intention.

8. Let your candle burn out, making sure it is attended to at all times, and leave your magical items in the jar for a day. When you take the items out, put your intention somewhere safe. You can leave your High Priestess card out and journal on it for a week, asking what message she has for you each day regarding your intuition or whatever comes up for you. Use your intuition crystal whenever you need a power boost.

———

Your experiences connecting with your intuition and psychic powers are going to be unique. Your connection to the crystals and the way you receive messages will feel and be different than other people's. That is why the best way to deepen your Crystal Enchanter craft is to experiment with the practice daily. See which exercises from this book (or ones that you develop yourself) create positive results. Keep track of your daily magical actions in your Crystal Enchanter spell book. Craft a mystical practice that brings you joy, one that taps into your intuitive magic and allows you to tune in with ease.

Chapter 9

Crystals for Peace and Calm

Who doesn't want to feel peace, bliss, and calming energy in their lives? In modern-day life, it seems like people feel they have to go, go, go. Everyone is so busy. There is so much to do and so little time. But when you don't make time for yourself to relax and chill, you wear yourself out and drain your energetic and physical bodies. This is especially true for parents because everyone in the household depends on them. I have lots of clients who are moms with kids that are running them ragged. I also see this in entrepreneurs, who are working so much that they do not have the time to relax. I can relate to this because I used to be like that too. I was an extreme workaholic; I just worked on my business and had no time for anything else.

Being busy and overwhelmed does not mean that you are productive. Having too much on your plate and feeling stressed can actually keep you stuck and blocked. There are times when people do work that is not even necessary because they feel the need to stay busy. This can stem from feelings of lack and insecurity. If your energy is calm and at peace, inspiration will come, opportunities will flow in, and you can work smarter, not harder.

I've noticed that if my clients do not take the time to take care of themselves and create a self-care routine or ritual, they end up burning out and crashing. In my experience, it often ends up with them getting an illness that forces them take a break. The Universe has been known to nudge people toward healing by making sure they have to rest, and you don't want to get to that point! Lucky for Crystal Enchanters, we know that there are crystals for everything, which means there are crystals that can infuse you with the energies of calm and peace. These crystals will work best if you pair them up with some kind of ritual or routine to invoke harmony into your life. Some of the things you can establish into your daily Crystal Enchanter practice are meditation, yoga, simple breath work, hypnosis, massage, taking naps, reading, energy healing, or whatever helps you feel relaxed.

Creating this calmness and stillness is a time to honor yourself and to honor your magic. Some of my clients tell me, "I don't have time. I am so busy." Want to know what I tell them? I tell them that is an excuse; it's just a story they've cultivated for themselves because they don't want to incorporate something new. People have time to scroll through the internet for hours each day, but they don't have time to work on their peace of mind for five minutes? Right ... I don't believe it. Prioritizing your peace is as important as prioritizing your physical health. When you are emotionally and physically healthy, you feel happy and have the energy to do whatever you desire.

In this chapter, you will be introduced to three of my favorite calming crystals—celestite, larimar, and blue calcite—to help you bring in the energy of peace. Everyone has their own interpretation of what it is like to feel peaceful. In my Crystal Enchanter practice, my definition of peaceful is feeling supported and at ease, like floating in a pool on a raft or sitting in a hammock and listening to the ocean crashing on the sand. It means having a clear mind, eliminating constant chatter and worry so that you are able to enjoy the moment and be fully present.

These peace and calming crystals have worked for me and my clients. Some of my clients have noticed a huge difference just by carrying a calming crystal with them every day. I had one girl tell me, "Oh my gosh, I forgot my crystal today, and I feel so weird without it." As you continue working with crystals, you will notice how you feel with and without them. Get ready to bring more peaceful energy into your life and to feel happiness and bliss.

EXERCISE
Mindfulness Magic

Many people practice mindfulness to acquire peace and calm, but mindfulness alone is not relaxation. When you are practicing mindfulness, you are fully aware or mindful of what you are thinking, doing, and being in the present moment. It is being aware of the now, and everything that is happening in your life, without judgment. Feeling relaxed and at peace can be a definite benefit of this practice. Here's an exercise to add to your Crystal Enchanter practice that cultivates focus, calm, and bliss using crystals and incorporates a powerful breathing exercise to enhance your mindfulness.

1. Find a sacred space that holds the energy of peace. Make sure it is someplace you won't be disturbed for the duration of your exercise. Set up and cleanse your area with sage, palo santo, or light from your heart, expanding the good

vibes throughout the room to clear away any energy that is negative or stagnant.

2. Get comfortable and lie down. Place the calm crystal that you have chosen for this exercise on your body. You can place it wherever is most comfortable for you; let your intuition guide you.

3. Focus on your breaths, slowly taking a deep inhale in and then letting a deep exhale out.

4. Clear your mind and focus on your breathing, feeling the weight of the crystal resting on you, calming you and filling you with peaceful energy.

5. Stay in this position and breathe for as long as you like, until your mind is clear and you feel calmness washing through you.

6. When you feel ready, feel the physical sensation of your body. Wiggle your toes and fingers. Pick up your crystal and hold it in your hands. Feel the temperature of the crystal. If it is cold, this could mean that the crystal assisted you in receiving good vibes and energy. If the crystal is hot, this could mean that the stones helped you release energy that is not needed.

7. Make sure to thank your crystal, your guides, and the Universe for their guidance, enjoying the peaceful energy and mindful of the energy around you.

In my experience, even if I take this time for myself for just three to five minutes a day, this magical practice helps me a lot. Working with calming and peaceful crystals can help you tap into that state of relaxation and recharge your battery. So set some time aside for a quick calming practice every day to center yourself. Also, treat yourself to a luxurious spa day at home or at a salon on occasion. I try to do this once a month or whenever my energy feels a bit low.

With the physical world moving at a faster pace, sometimes it is hard to slow down and relax. When dogs are barking, kids need to be fed, and there is work to do, taking time for yourself seems to be at the bottom of the to-do list. Being a Crystal Enchanter is all about being consciously aware of your energies and what is going on around you. Not taking time to replenish your energy or doing a calming practice can leave you feeling depleted. And how can you help others if you have no energy left?

• Celestite •

Important Crystal Note: Celestite in its raw cluster form crumbles and breaks off, so use the indirect method from chapter 12 for crafting crystal potions. Also, make sure to keep this crystal out of the sun so it doesn't lose its gorgeous baby blue color.

Celestite is a beautiful, angelic blue crystal that holds the energy of heavenly peace. Not only does it bring a sense of unity and belonging in this world, but this gem can help you connect with the angelic realm and assist in your communications with your guardian angels and spirit guides. When celestite is in its raw geode form, sometimes it looks like a small cave. The points look like glittering lights. This is my favorite blue crystal. The most common colors of celestite are pale blue, baby blue, or blue-gray. When I go on my crystal buying trips, I like to search for those that are a beautiful baby blue color. Those that hold the nice heavenly blue color are usually higher in quality. Celestite is not a hard crystal, so be careful when handling it because it does crumble easily. Also, don't leave celestite in the sun or under strong lamplight for long because the crystal will lose its gorgeous color.

The energy of this crystal is a soft but powerful frequency that sends out the feeling of being at peace and calm. This blue crystal can activate your throat chakra to help you speak your truth. When you are expressing your truth confidently and have excellent communication and understanding with others, this usually brings peace into your life. Celestite is also a unique healing mineral to have in your Crystal Enchanter magical toolbox because it can clear and heal the aura and assist in balancing your energies, helping you feel centered. Keep a celestite geode in your living room or office to relieve tension and promote a happy, calm, and positive environment for everyone.

A Channeled Message from the Celestite Collective

"Like the rolling of the soft clouds in the sky, roll roll roll through your life with ease. When you see a thunderstorm coming, embrace it with all you've got, and soon it shall pass. Let the coolness of the breeze help you feel blissful and blow away anything that is not needed. When you are genuinely at peace, your body, mind, and spirit will float."

Emotional Healing

Celestite can uplift your emotional well-being. If you are feeling negative and down, this gem can help you shift to a higher level of emotional frequency.

Celestite promotes the energetic vibrations of calm and peace. You can place celestite in a community room where everyone hangs out to enhance the energies of harmony in that space.

This gem can also enhance mental clarity and the ability to stay calm while finding the solution to a challenging situation. When you are at peace, your mind is clearer, and this allows your subconscious mind and intuition to be heard and better support you on your journey.

Magical Uses

- Work with your celestite when you are tapping into the angelic realm, channeling the angels, or connecting with your spirit guides. You will notice that messages and downloads will be more precise if you are holding on to a celestite crystal.

- If you would like to astral travel, celestite can help keep you safe during your travels and the initial departure. This crystal can also help you remember your astral travel or dreams if you keep one under your pillow or bed.

- Celestite enhances your intuitive abilities and psychic powers. It can amplify your clairvoyance and clairaudience so that you are more open to receiving messages.

Crystal Affirmation: "I Am at Peace with Myself and My Life"

Recite this affirmation while looking at yourself in the mirror. The mirror can be small and handheld or another mirror of your choosing. Look into your own eyes as you recite this crystal affirmation. Say "I am at peace with myself and my life" and believe that the person looking back at you through the mirror feels that way. With each breath and each repetition, you will see the affirmation infuse into your soul through your eyes. Say this affirmation until you feel it in your body and confirm it with your reflection. You will know when you are ready to stop.

Crystal Tip
Celestite Selection

I've seen many celestite crystals, especially on buying trips at crystal shows. They are pretty common, so I want to make sure that you select a celestite of awesome quality and vibration. My goal when I shop is to select the crystals that are the most beautiful and have the best energy. I feel like the look of the crystals has a lot to do with the magic that they exude. If the crystal is damaged or mined poorly, this could affect its power and energetic frequency. However, each crystal is unique, and different people love different styles. So the most important thing is that it looks beautiful to you and has qualities that you love. A chipped crystal does not mean that it is terrible; sometimes this chip gives it character.

Choosing a high-quality celestite is very easy to do. When you go celestite hunting, you will want to look for specific qualities to pick out a high-quality gem. The first thing to look for is its form. My shop usually buys celestite in its raw form, which means that it has a cluster of points still in the geode, connected to rock on the bottom or back. I love the natural look of these crystals because I haven't come across any polished celestite that I have loved. When celestite is polished, I feel like it takes away the sparkle and shine of the crystal. With that being said, you need to see for yourself what you like!

The second thing to look for is the color. Celestite comes in a heavenly pale blue that is translucent. Look for the deeper blues for higher quality. Sometimes a clear celestite speaks to me, though, and it may to you. Just be sure the crystal points look "clean" and not muddled; then it should be a good quality stone. Also, make sure there are no dirt stains on the blue parts. However, there are times when a crystal winks at you. No matter what it looks like, if you feel a connection, you better take that baby home because you are supposed to work with it somehow!

Thirdly, and most importantly, make sure your celestite is not crumbling. If you notice that pieces of your stone are breaking off, that probably means a more significant part of the crystal will break off at some point. I would pass on a crumbled celestite unless you are super careful with it, can take it home straight away, and can put it somewhere it won't be disturbed. Once, I bought a beautiful celestite that was crumbling because it was just too beautiful not to buy. By the time I got home, the celestite had already broken in half even though I was super cautious with it.

Now you are an expert at acquiring a high-vibe celestite for your Crystal Enchanter collection. Can't wait to see what you find!

• Larimar •

Important Crystal Note: Keep this crystal out of the sun so it doesn't lose its gorgeous color.

Larimar is a rare blue pectolite only found in the Dominican Republic, which is in the Caribbean. My first encounter with larimar was when my friend came back from the Dominican Republic with a delightful crystal ring. I was drawn to the ring and the soothing energies the stone was emitting, and she told me that it is an exceptional crystal only found there. When you look at larimar, it's like looking at the waters of the Caribbean. There is a mix of light blue, blue and white, and green blue to deep blue. Sometimes you can find hematite inclusions or brown oxidations in the stone. The deeper and more intense the blue color of the crystal, the more value it has. Make sure to keep this rare crystal out of the sun so that the precious blue color does not fade.

Larimar is sometimes known as the Atlantean stone, referring to the connection of magic between the people of Atlantis and the power of the sea. Another name for larimar is the dolphin stone. It is said that if you meditate with larimar and the music of the dolphin calls, you can call upon the swift healing energies of the dolphin collectives.

When you carry this gem, you will feel complete and inner calmness that will allow you to connect to the flow of life. Although this crystal is not as common as clear quartz or amethyst, it is still very common in shops. Most metaphysical or online crystal shops have larimar in stock. Once you see this crystal, whether on the internet or in person, you will likely be inspired by its beauty and be drawn into its healing energies.

Also, as an example of magical Crystal Enchanter synchronicity, as I was writing about larimar, someone who does a form of Atlantean healing messaged me out of the blue. What confirmation!

A Channeled Message from the Larimar Collective

"From the ocean, from the sea, onto land, and into your home. Rest in the waves and float to your next destination. Let the dolphins chatter and guide you swiftly to your goals. The sea is mysterious and has secrets that we cannot fully uncover. When new discoveries are made, it can be strange but also very beautiful. What secrets do you need to discover? What mysteries do you need to reveal and wash away before you can reach your inner peace and float amongst the waves?"

Emotional Healing

Like all the calming crystals in this chapter, larimar can also help you release stress and anxiety. Larimar uses the loving, healing energy of the ocean to do so. You will feel like you are floating on waves of love or swinging stress-free in a hammock on the beach.

Larimar gives you strength, courage, and emotional stability. It will instill you with the power of clear communication to allow you to speak your truth and feel at peace with your choices.

If you are feeling impatient and always on the run, larimar can help slow down that energy and teach you about patience and respect. When you let things grow in alignment with divine timing, you will see that the wait is necessary and always worth it. The end result will be better than you had imagined.

Magical Uses

- Larimar is a singer's talisman because the blue stone can activate your throat chakra and unleash your true voice to be shared with the world. The energy of this gem can also protect your vocal cords and enhance the power of your voice.

- My favorite magical mermaid stone to work with is larimar. When I am tapping into the enchantment of the sea or connecting to my mermaid guides, I love to hold on to larimar as I work. When I am holding larimar, I can feel the refreshing spray of the ocean and sometimes even smell the salt water.

- This beautiful crystal can also help soul mates find one another. That seems to be one of larimar's most well-known magical properties. Keep the crystal with you or in your bedroom. Not only can you use this to find your soul mate, but larimar will also heal any negative karma between you and others because it allows you to have open communication with people you have a relationship with.

Crystal Affirmation: "Relaxation Washes Over Me with Every Breath I Take"

Recite this crystal affirmation throughout the day whenever you feel out of balance or overwhelmed. Say "Relaxation washes over me with every breath I take" out loud or in your mind. As you are saying it, feel a gentle, warm wave of relaxation wash over you as you breathe in. Take a moment and sit in the stillness of this calm energy as it recharges your body, mind, and soul. I like to set an alarm for the middle of the day to remind myself to do my breathing ritual. If this is something that resonates with you, you can add this affirmation and process into your daily routine or ritual.

Crystal Tip
Animal Peace

Did you know that crystal energy affects animals too? Yes, it does! Your pets and animals might be even more sensitive to a crystal's energy than you are, so you can use crystal magic to help heal them. When my crystal clients have trouble handling their animals, like if the pet is too rowdy or pets are fighting with each other, I always suggest incorporating larimar.

One of my clients who sheltered dogs was housing two pups that did not like each other. She tried to keep them apart, but somehow they would always find a way to break free and get into a fight. Thankfully, the physical fights were not serious. It was mostly just the dogs barking at each other, but the barking got on everyone's nerves. I was playing with my larimar the day that she presented this problem to me, so I told her to get larimar and put it by each of the dogs. Like an obsessed crystal lover, she had two larimar crystals. She set one by each of the dogs and that day, there was no barking wildly at each other! We still had no idea what problem they had with each other, but we knew that the calming energy of the larimar gently settled them down. They both looked super happy, tranquil, and content. It was an amazing experience for all of us, and ever since then, I have suggested larimar to calm down animals.

You can also use crystals to help calm babies and toddlers. The best crystal to keep them at peace is celestite. I've never tried putting celestite and larimar together before, but it probably would be super powerful. If you try this, make sure to let me know how it turns out.

If you are faced with either of these challenges, now you know what to do!

• Blue Calcite •

Last but not least, another crystal that assists in bringing peace and has a calming effect is blue calcite. These peaceful crystals are great gifts because this gem is so easy to work with and has a gentle healing energy. When you work with this crystal, you get lulled into the blissful energy that blue calcite emits to promote instant healing. There are tons of calcite crystals. They are all different colors depending on the minerals that are present in the stone. Similar to other calcite crystals, blue calcite is made up of calcium carbonate and other minerals that produce the sky blue color. The extra minerals in the calcite change the energy and magic of the crystal.

Some people get calcite crystals and quartz mixed up. The easiest way to identify calcites is to look for a sheen of shine on its surface with a texture that is almost waxy or soapy. Although the healing energy from this stone is gentle, it is still a potent stone for soothing and relaxing the mind, body, and spirit. This calcite, with the gorgeous blue hue at its core, is the stone for communication because it is related to the throat chakra. Having this crystal around you can help calm the chatter in your mind to lift your energetic frequency higher, especially during a meditation. Blue calcite will allow you to enhance your communication with others and guide you to speak your truth and express your emotions.

In my Crystal Enchanter practice, I love to work with the raw form of this stone the most, and I hold it in my palms as I meditate. Experiment with your gems and see how you best connect with crystal magic.

A Channeled Message from the Blue Calcite Collective

"Like the blue jays in the sky, our energy is here to bring you joy, lightness, and peace. Have you ever found serenity just sitting outside and listening to the birds? Feel the sun and wind caressing your skin, experience stillness, and bring your awareness to the energies surrounding you and within you. This is contentment; this is bliss. If you haven't tried this, we encourage you to go into your yard, a park, or a forest and just sit in peace for as long as you can and enjoy that magical moment."

Emotional Healing

This gorgeous blue crystal assists in relaxation by absorbing stress, anxiety, and any other negative emotions from you. Blue calcite alchemizes negative emotions and sends them back to you with positive, uplifting vibes.

Blue calcite can inspire motivation and create forward momentum by assisting you in letting go of old, negative emotional patterns and increasing your drive to succeed.

The energy of the blue calcite is very loving and comforting, so if you are ever experiencing emotional distress or a breakdown, hold on to your crystal and imagine everything that you are feeling at that moment flowing into the stone. Then imagine positive, peaceful vibes flowing back out, surrounding your whole body with a calming energy.

Magical Uses

- Placing blue calcite in your most-used rooms, especially rooms where people gather, can promote blissful and peaceful energy. The energy of this stone can repel negative energy and chase it out of your space.

- Many of the crystal vendors at shows that I've been to have told me that blue calcite crystals are used to develop psychic powers, especially telepathy. I have not personally tried to use blue calcite to develop telepathy, but this makes sense since it is a communication stone.

- If you are stuck in a creative block, blue calcite can be used to inspire you and help you push through the stagnant energy. This crystal will allow you to download the creative ideas and messages that are divinely for you, so it is also perfect for busting through writer's block.

Crystal Affirmation: "I Am Relaxed and Empowered throughout the Day"

Recite this crystal affirmation as soon as you wake up in the morning. You can say this to yourself as you are lying in your bed, not even fully awake. Program this affirmation into your mind, energy, and body for the rest of the day. Right before you sleep and right when you wake up are the easiest times to program the mind. As you say this affirmation, feel yourself relaxing deeply, full of magic, knowing your day will be fantastic. Do this for as long as you want. However, sometimes I fall back asleep while reciting this affirmation, so make sure your snooze alarm is on!

Crystal Tip
Technology Magic

As you know, blue calcite opens up the throat chakra and allows you to speak your truth. It allows you to communicate your emotions and desires in a way that others will understand. The throat chakra is the control center of your body that deals with communication. Having a balanced and healed throat chakra can result in your ability to speaking clearer, with confidence, and to be able to articulate your ideas and feelings. Nowadays, most people communicate through some sort of technological device like a phone or computer.

Whether you are speaking into the phone, texting a message, or sending an email, these are all forms of communication. There is energy being sent back and forth from you to the other person through electronic technology. Have you ever noticed that sometimes the true meaning of words gets lost in a text or email, especially when it's something important, and you can come off as aggressive or uncaring to the other person because they misunderstood the message? Some people don't express their feelings well over text, but blue calcite can help you out with that.

This magical crystal can help you formulate the right words and sentences to type so that the other person understands them. Blue calcite can help get your point across in an essential message without offending the other person in any way. So, when you are typing a vital email or text, make sure you have your blue calcite somewhere nearby and invoke its magical communicative power to help you out.

EXERCISE
Crystal Breathing

Breathing is a vital part of living. Breath work has lots of health benefits; it can help bring peace to the mind and calm the body and soul. I've noticed that a lot of my students do not breathe properly or do not take time to do intentional breathing during the day. Although breathing with your crystal can help you connect to its energy and infuse its magic into every cell of your body, taking intentional breaths with your crystal can elevate and enhance your experience even further.

First, choose a crystal that you would like to work with. It should be a crystal with the energy that matches the intention you are setting for this exercise. For example, if you are calling in calming energy, you could choose celestite because of its calming and peaceful energy.

Hold your crystal in the palm of your hand and focus on your connection with the crystal. Close your eyes and feel or see bright energy flowing from the crystal to you through your hands. Now you can start your breathing. Breathe in for ten seconds, hold your breath for ten seconds, then release for ten seconds. Do this for three minutes. If you cannot inhale for ten seconds, try for five seconds each round. If you have mastered the ten seconds, try to go for fifteen or twenty seconds. Let each breath fill your lungs with the energy of the crystal. As you breathe in, your belly and lungs should expand as the energy of the crystal fills you up. As you exhale, push all the air out, navel to spine, and feel the energy of the crystal disperse throughout your whole body. Inhale good vibes and exhale all your stress, frustration, and anxiety.

This crystal breathing exercise can be done anywhere! If you feel overwhelmed at work, just step out, sit in your car, and breathe through this simple and magical exercise.

Crystal Calming Spell

This crystal calming spell is to help you feel relaxed, at peace, and supported. You can use this spell when you feel anxious, worried, or nervous before a big event. The spell is perfect for performers or speakers, and you could even do this spell before a job interview or when your nerves are getting to you. Perform this spell at least one day before your event, and believe that you will accomplish your goal with ease.

Magical Tools
Calming crystal
A piece of fruit or candy
Blue candle and matches or a lighter

1. Create your intention and set up your sacred space.
2. Tune in by closing your eyes and focusing on your breath, breathing evenly and deeply with each inhale and exhale.

3. Light your blue candle and say this opening prayer: "I light this candle to calm my mind, body, and spirit. And so it shall be."

4. Hold your crystal in your right hand and your fruit or candy in your left hand. Hold them out in front of you and say, "Piece by piece, I am at peace. Imbue this fruit/candy with harmony, light, and bliss for stress, anxiety, and fear. I will now dismiss, and so it is."

5. Imagine a blue healing light traveling from your hand holding the crystal into the other hand holding your fruit or candy, infusing your fruit or candy with the blissful magic of the crystal.

6. When you think you are done with the infusion of power, eat your fruit or candy and say, "I am at peace."

7. Let your candle burn all the way down to complete the spell. You can use a birthday candle for faster burning if you do not have a lot of time. Make sure you don't leave the candle unattended; extinguish the flame if you are not around.

As you can see, there are many easy crystal spells and exercises that you can incorporate into your life to help you call in energies of peace and tranquility. Allow yourself to reset and regenerate in the still moments you have created so that you can always show up as your best self. The best way to do this is to incorporate some sort of calming ritual or habit daily. Make this a part of your routine and the other everyday habits you may have, such as making the bed. Remember, magic can be simple, so set a specific time during the day to do a little bit of crystal magic and to refresh your body, mind, and soul.

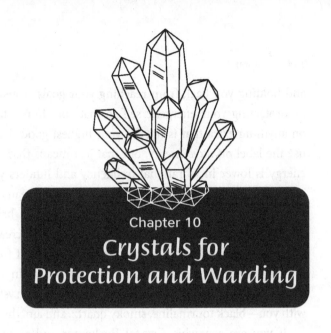

Chapter 10
Crystals for Protection and Warding

In this chapter, I introduce the top three crystals in my Crystal Enchanter collection for protection and warding. First, let's clarify what you will be protecting yourself or your space from. You will be clearing energy that brings you to a lower vibe and energy you do not need in your life. When your energy is not up to par or when you are in low-vibrational frequency, it doesn't mean that you are a low-vibe person, it just means that there are some blockages and imbalances that need to be cleared so that you can start attracting the things you desire. These vibrational energies that are dragging you down will be blocking you and holding you back from reaching your goals. You will be protecting your energetic self so that you do not take on anything extra that is not for your highest good. I will use the label *negative energy*, but that just means that this energy is lower in vibrational frequency and hinders you more than it helps you. Negative energy does not mean bad energy; energy is just energy. Negative energy can bring about negative thoughts and feelings, which then creates a reality to match it. That is why protecting yourself from drawing in negative energies is very important. In this chapter, I will be sharing three powerful protection crystals with you—black tourmaline, smoky quartz, and amethyst.

If you are a newbie Crystal Enchanter and/or often feel overwhelmed by other people's energies, then protection crystals are the perfect crystals to keep with you at all times. One of my clients used to get horrible headaches and emotional mood swings daily. She said she was sensitive to the energies around her and always picked up on other people's negative energies. This client had yet to learn how to control her empathic abilities, so she was unintentionally taking on other people's energies. I shared these three protection crystals with my empathic crystal client. I also told her how to do an aura energy protection ritual before going out (this will be shared with you in the next exercise). She began performing the ritual daily and carrying a protection crystal in her bra before she went out and noticed a positive change. Although there was more magical work that she had to do, she felt a lot better after incorporating these two energetic practices. Even if this is the first time you are working with crystals or magic, they can improve many areas of your life. For example, once you learn how to protect your energy, it is effortless to do so and other people's energy will stop bothering you. Until you do learn this, though, you can invoke the magic of one of these protection crystals to help you out.

What I love about protection and warding crystals is that, while they work with our energies automatically, they are even more powerful when we infuse them with intention and give them a specific direction. That is why you should always activate your crystals or ask them to help you. My favorite way of working with protection crystals is to put some by the front door of my house. This deters anyone who has lower-vibrational energy or intent from coming to my house. I recommend this practice to many of my clients. You can even put protection crystals in your car to help prevent break-ins.

Hopefully, these stories and the information I share about these crystals will inspire you to add a protection crystal to your Crystal Enchanter collection. Do this chapter's protection exercise to create a safe and high-vibe reality for you and your loved ones.

• Black Tourmaline •

Important Crystal Note: Black tourmaline contains aluminum, so you should use the indirect method from chapter 12 for creating crystal potions. It is safe to handle and work with in your other magical practices. A bit of a warning: raw black tourmaline crystals are pretty fragile; they can get crumbly and break off easily. Tumbled black tourmaline is safe to put in water, but do not put raw tourmaline in water.

Black tourmaline is part of the tourmaline family, and it is a very popular varietal in the crystal collectors' world. Tourmaline is beautiful and powerful, and you can find it in black, pink, green, yellow, brown, blue, red, and violet. Sometimes it can even merge and create the exquisite watermelon tourmaline, which has pink and green tourmaline together. Black tourmaline can come in many forms, but my favorite is a chunky, gorgeous raw tourmaline. Sometimes quartz, mica, and other unusual minerals can be found growing with the black tourmaline.

Raw black tourmaline can be crumbly and spindly, much like kyanite crystals. High-quality tourmaline is smooth, but the price will reflect that. No matter the quality of your black tourmaline, its energy works the same. In the crystal healing world, black tourmaline is very well-known for its protective qualities of repelling negative energy, dispelling negative beliefs and emotions, and purifying one's thoughts.

Black tourmaline is one of the main crystals I use when I need to ground. Let's say you are accessing your third eye and working with divine energies. Sometimes it is hard to come back to the present in the physical world. That is where the black tourmaline comes in, as this stone will help you ground yourself in the present moment and the here and now.

When you are feeling stagnant, unlucky, or unsure of what you are doing, you can use the magic of black tourmaline to help you out. I had a friend who was in town to play in a poker tournament, and she told me to give her a crystal to help her win. Now, I usually would've given her a prosperity and money stone, but this little black tourmaline wanted to go to her. Like an intuitive Crystal Enchanter, I listened to my crystal and trusted that she needed this rock. It turns out it did help her. She ended up making money gambling and did pretty well in the tournament. So you see, black tourmaline is not just about protecting your energy and space. If you feel protected and supported, then you will be able to trust yourself and confidently reach your goals.

A Channeled Message from the Black Tourmaline Collective

"The black in our crystal mineral sparkles in the sun, and if you study it carefully, you will see we are not just a flat black. As black tourmaline, we clear and wash away negative energy, leaving you with a clean, shiny slate. That is all we do, and we wash away the energies that are not needed anymore. After you are cleansed and centered back to your zero point, it is up to you to call in the energy of your choosing. So, what will you decide to call in? What will you focus on? Hopefully we do not need to wash you clean too often."

Emotional Healing

If you feel like someone is causing you distress or draining your energy whenever you are near them, wear a black tourmaline (or stick one in your pocket or bra) to create an energetic boundary and protect your energy.

When you are confused or stuck during a situation or challenge, call on your black tourmaline for help. This gem should clear away the fog and help you discover the answers that you need to move forward.

Black tourmaline can cleanse and purify feelings of unworthiness, fear, doubt, anxiety, depression, and anger. Hold on to your crystal and breathe, letting the healing energies of the stone wash away your worries.

Magical Uses

- Like I have mentioned before, after meditation or a spiritual journey, use black tourmaline to ground yourself in the present before you do anything else (like operating a vehicle) so that you are entirely in your physical body and the present moment.

- If you are an urban Crystal Enchanter, you are around lots of technology and pollution. Black tourmaline can help protect you from electromagnetic fields, radiation, and environmental pollutions.

- Use black tourmaline during root chakra healing and meditation work. This crystal will enhance the magic and energies of your practice, providing magical protection around you.

Crystal Affirmation: "I Am Safe and Protected in Every Way"

When your world feels a little shaken up and you need some magical assurance, recite this crystal affirmation as you hold on your protection crystal to your heart. As you are saying "I am safe and protected in every way," imagine a beautiful white light surrounding you and protecting you from any negative energies. Just saying this affirmation three times while visualizing the healing light can immediately help you feel balanced and supported.

Crystal Tip
Online Shopping Enchantment

I am one of those people who hates going out to shop, so I do all my shopping online. I love online shopping; it is perfect for the introverted Crystal Enchanter that I am. I also make a lot of packages for my crystal shop and my tarot deck, so people shop online and purchase things from me. You are probably wondering how crystals and magic relate to online shopping. Well, let me share with you how I use black tourmaline to help my online business, especially when I need to send items out. Lucky you, you will be receiving three tips in one!

The first tip is that when you are online shopping for a rare item and you have to bid for it, it's being restocked, or there is a limited amount, black tourmaline can help you get the item you desire. Before I go online to bid for a rare item or pop in for the inventory drop, I have my trusty black tourmaline with me. I tell the crystal precisely what it is that I am shopping for and imagine that item in my hands. Then I am to be prepared to take action. Be ready at the time of the drop or auction, and be confident that you will win. Most of the time, I win my auctions and get the items that I want.

The second tip is about protecting packages left at your house. If you love online shopping, you probably receive a lot of packages that get left at your front door. If you are not home often, you will want those packages to be protected. To protect your packages and your home, put four small black tourmaline crystals underneath your welcome mat, one under each of the four corners. I use super cheap, three-dollar baby ones for this. You don't need to splurge on crystals for their magic to work. The crystals in the four corners will form an energetic protective field around your home and protect you and your packages. I've never gotten a package stolen before, but I still use this practice because it's better to be safe than sorry!

The third tip is about making sure whatever you are shipping gets to its destination safely. When I am sending something special or expensive to my clients, I put a black tourmaline crystal on top of the package and set an intention for safe and swift travels before mailing it. You can also sprinkle black tourmaline dust in the package itself or put a little one inside. If you own some black tourmaline already, you can retrieve the dust for free. It's normal for these stones to crumble and to leave black tourmaline dust. Don't throw the crumbles or dust away—use them to bless your packages!

There you go. Now your online shopping will be blessed, safe, and protected. Happy shopping!

• Amethyst •

Amethyst is like the queen of crystals to me. It is part of the quartz family and is related to the clear quartz. You can use amethyst for almost anything in life, and it is so accessible. It is one of the most popular crystals out there. I think it's because the energy of this stone is powerful without being overpowering, and it is super easy to work with. No matter what, this is a crystal you need to get for your Crystal Enchanter collection. This gorgeous purple gem can come in clusters, terminated points, and geodes.

Whether the crystal is raw or polished, amethyst is equally beautiful. My favorite type of amethyst is a cluster, shaped like a half-circle dome and looking like a rose. The amount of iron in the crystal is what determines the intensity of its purple color. Amethyst can be a royal purple, lavender, part white, and even transparent. Although amethyst is a powerful protection and warding crystal, this stone can be used for many magical things. One of the most popular energetic uses of the amethyst is to awaken and enhance psychic powers. This crystal can help you tap into your intuition, activating the third eye and invoking your magic, all the while protecting you from harm. What a fantastic crystal!

I love to have amethyst around my work desk to help inspire creativity for my projects. The divine energy of this stone will create a protective energy shield around your mind, body, and spirit, assisting you in releasing negative energies and thoughts. Grab yourself an amethyst crystal and claim the magic it has in store for you.

A Channeled Message from the Amethyst Collective

"Divine for inspiration from the stars and ground the energy into the body to manifest your dreams in your physical world. Divining comes from your heart center and expands out into the Universe to receive creative ideas that will guide you to your goal. When you are supported, when you feel the love in your heart, that is when you can easily connect to this divine energy, call forth ideas, and manifest your desires into reality. When you are full of love, you are fully protected. When you trust, your third eye is activated. Work with amethyst and open your heart, intuition, and magic to receive the guidance that is fully aligned with you."

Emotional Healing

A naturally stress-relieving crystal, amethyst can help you release tension and calm the mind. Carry an amethyst with you if you are having a challenging time for protection and peace of mind.

The healing energy of this crystal can help alleviate the addiction to harmful habits. This can also apply to addictive negative thoughts that you project in your mind constantly.

If you are feeling negative about yourself or your life, working with the healing energies of the amethyst can help you move toward feeling neutral about things—and perhaps even feeling happy—in the near future.

Magical Uses

- Amethyst can supposedly prevent you from getting drunk. There is a legend that if you drink from an amethyst-encrusted cup, you cannot get intoxicated, but what is the fun in that, right? When my friends are hungover, I suggest they carry around an amethyst if they feel like crap. Mystics have also worn amethyst rings to keep from getting spiritually drunk so that they are grounded and centered.

- Place an amethyst crystal on your third eye to activate your psychic powers and to enhance your intuition. You can do this before divining or performing a ritual and spell.

- Put an amethyst under your pillow or near your bed to promote a good night's rest. Your magical purple crystal can help fight off insomnia and protect you from bad dreams. If you wish, you can also use amethyst to help you recall your

dreams by setting an intention with your crystal
before you go to bed.

Crystal Affirmation: "I Am Divinely Protected at All Times"

Recite this affirmation as you hold on to your amethyst
crystal to call in protection from the Universe, angels,
guardian angels, or whomever you divine with. Activate
the power of the amethyst at any time to request protection from the divine. You can use this affirmation before
performing a magical spell, ritual, or reading. This is also
a potent affirmation to invoke before astral traveling to
protect your spirit and body.

Crystal Tip
Ametrine

There are many different kinds of amethyst available.
They are all beautiful and filled with healing magic. One
of my favorite amethysts in my collection is a small, transparent, lavender tower with rainbow inclusions. Another
extraordinary type of amethyst is called *ametrine*, also
known as *trystine*. This crystal is amethyst that naturally
grew together with citrine. Ametrine towers are potent
magical tools for manifestation and spells. This is not a
super common crystal, but if you do stumble across one,

make sure that it is translucent, with the combination of purple and light yellow or brown throughout the crystal.

As you know, amethyst is for protection, to activate psychic powers, and so much more. Citrine is for abundance, joy, and energy. Combining the two creates a super-magical crystal that can help you accomplish just about any goal. Ametrine is known to help you release your addictions, enhance your intuition, and provide mental clarity. It can also help with weight loss. When amethyst and citrine combine, the energies in the crystals are amped up and balance each other really well. You tap into the higher frequencies of crown and third eye chakras with the amethyst and the energies of the lower chakras, the solar plexus and sacral, with the citrine. This connection will assist you in bringing your thoughts and intentions into reality by working with both the spiritual and the physical realm. Of course, having both citrine and amethyst in your Crystal Enchanter collection would be magical enough, but if you do happen to see an ametrine, I suggest you pick it up and see if it is winking at you.

• Smoky Quartz •

Important Crystal Note: Natural smoky quartz is nontoxic and great for crystal potions using the direct method. Artificial smoky quartz that has a deep black color is usually irradiated. There are crystal dealers that irradiate clear quartz to create a manmade smoky quartz that can be hard to distinguish from the real thing. Both are equally magical for me, but the artificial smoky quartz should be handled with caution when creating crystal potions or anything for ingestion. I suggest using the indirect method from chapter 12 for your craft just to be on the safe side.

Smoky quartz is also known as the wishing stone or the manifesting stone because it does what the name says—it manifests your wishes. This translucent brownish-gray or black crystal is also a member of the quartz family. The smoky colors occur with natural irradiation and contains aluminum. When I introduce beginner Crystal Enchanters to crystals, I make sure to suggest this stone because it is a powerful protective and grounding crystal. Plus, who wouldn't want a crystal that will make their wishes come true?! As with the other black crystals, you can also use smoky quartz to clear electromagnetic pollution and return it safely to the earth.

Smoky quartz comes in many forms. My favorite are smoky quartz clusters, especially the baby ones because they are just so cute. If you only want natural crystals, make sure that you ask if it is a natural black-colored quartz when you purchase smoky quartz; sometimes the gorgeous, deep-black ones are manmade. Manmade and natural smoky quartz do have the same energy, and I work with both. The most important thing when you use a crystal is your intention.

If you are looking to make your wishes come true and stay protected as you work your magic, add a beautiful smoky quartz to your Crystal Enchanter collection.

A Channeled Message from the Smoky Quartz Collective

"Buried in the deep of the earth is where you will discover us. We are imbued with so much earth magic that sometimes it can make you dizzy, but not us! Our energy is stable, our energy is grounding, and our magic will help you stay in the present and conscious of this world. All living things have roots, energetic roots, that are drawn from the earth. These energetic roots can help you heal, ground, and feel protected at all times. Activate the magic of us, the smoky quartz, and we will help you be aware of these roots and expand the flow of the protective energies into your vessel. Know that you are always rooted, always protected, and always safe. No matter where you are or what you are doing, just believe."

Emotional Healing

If you feel like a negative black cloud is hanging over your head, hold on to smoky quartz and ask this crystal to transmute that energy into positive vibes.

When brought to the workplace, smoky quartz can help uplift the mood. This grounding crystal can resolve anger and miscommunication in the workplace and protect you against hurtful, annoying gossip.

You can call upon the magic of the smoky quartz to help you bust through negative emotions or emotional blockages, allowing positive thoughts and feelings to replace them.

Magical Uses

- Like all black or brown crystals, this crystal has a strong connection to earth magic. Smoky quartz will help you ground, stay present, and come back to your physical reality.

- To supercharge your new moon intentions, add smoky quartz to your manifesting ritual or create a crystal grid with it. The crystal will guide you. It helps you move toward your goals with clarity.

- This powerful crystal can help you manifest personal or business intentions. Smoky quartz can attract abundance and protection to all areas of your life.

Crystal Affirmation: "I Am Grounded, Safe, and Supported"

Recite this affirmation with your smoky quartz underneath your pillow before you go to bed. It will ensure a good night's sleep by helping you feel grounded, safe, and supported. This imprints the words and the energy into your subconscious mind and every cell of your body as you sleep. You will likely wake up feeling better than ever, knowing that you are protected. This will help you have the courage to pursue your goals.

Crystal Tip
Travel Protection

Many crystals can protect you when you are traveling, whether you are just driving to work or flying overseas for an amazing adventure. If you are a wanderlust Crystal Enchanter, having smoky quartz in your collection would be smart. This black crystal is an amazing protective stone while traveling. Whenever I am flying, I always make sure I take a smoky quartz crystal with me on the flight. It helps me feel protected, safe, and grounded, even if I am in the air.

It is perfectly legal and safe to take crystals with you on an airplane. My suggestion is to keep the crystal in your carry-on bag first, then transfer it to your bra or somewhere on your body after going through TSA and the security checkpoint. I've been stopped and checked there before because my crystal registered on the screen. Once when I had the crystal in my bra, TSA was curious about what it was. After I took it out and showed them, they laughed and let me pass. I've also put crystals in my pocket and been stopped by TSA. So, if you do not want to be stopped at security, start with it in your bag.

If you are carrying large crystals in your carry-on, airport security might also pull your bag over to the side and check it. I've checked in loads of crystals as gifts, and that was okay. However, keeping larger crystals in your luggage will probably be safest if you pack them well.

Have fun on your next adventure, and make sure to grab smoky quartz before you leave the house. However, if you are someone that tends to lose things on trips, you might want to grab a cheaper smoky quartz to take with you on your adventures!

EXERCISE
Root Magic

The feelings of being safe, supported, and protected all reside in the root chakra. If your root chakra is out of balance or blocked with memories or experiences from the past when you did not feel protected, then this could lead to you feeling unsafe in the present. Almost everything that makes us feel unworthy, afraid, or doubtful boils down to healing the root chakra. To cultivate a strong belief about being safe and supported that will allow you to accomplish many things in your life, add this root magic exercise to your Crystal Enchanter rituals. Do this every day, every week, or whenever you are called to clear negative emotions and beliefs.

1. Create a sacred, comfortable space that will allow you to perform this exercise without being interrupted. You can do this first thing when you wake up, during the day, or before you go to sleep—whatever feels best for you.

2. Make sure that you are holding your favorite protection crystal during this exercise. You will be putting your crystal on your root chakra, which is at the base of your spine, during the practice. If you are sitting in a chair, you may place the crystal on your lap close to the front of your root chakra. If you are lying down, you can place the crystal on top of your clothing in the root chakra area.

3. Close your eyes and tune in to your breath, breathing deeply and evenly through your nose. Keep your focus up toward your third eye, which is in the middle of your forehead, to activate your magic.

4. Imagine a strong cord connecting your root chakra to the center of the earth, anchoring itself onto a giant crystal and drawing up the healing energies through the cord and into your root chakra. As you breathe deeper and deeper, you will notice a red light at your root chakra that is growing bigger and bigger.

5. As you are drawing up this grounding, healing energy, say, "I am safe. I am protected. I am supported." Keep repeating this for one to three minutes.

6. When you feel like you are safe, protected, and warm all over, go ahead and visualize pulling up your anchor. Slowly draw the imagined cord back into your root chakra. Imagine the red ball of energy getting smaller and smaller, shrinking down to its standard size.

7. When you are ready to come back to the physical world, take a deep breath in through your nose and exhale out through your mouth loudly. Wiggle your fingers, wiggle your toes, and open your eyes, feeling whole, safe, and protected.

Crystal Protection Spell

This crystal protection spell is used to guard a physical item such as yourself, your space, or an item. You are putting magical, sparkly energy around anything you want to be protected. This crystal spell will help you ward off negative energy and people so that your possessions and your body will be safe and protected. Make sure you are also making smart decisions and taking action in your everyday life to stay safe and well.

Magical Tools

Protection crystal

Black candle and matches or a lighter

Salt

1. Create your intention and set up your sacred space.

2. Tune in by closing your eyes and focusing on your breath, breathing evenly and deeply with each inhale and exhale.

3. Light your black candle. Take your protection crystal and move it over the flame three times. Do not let your crystal touch the flame. Hold it just slightly above the flame, and be careful not to burn yourself! Move the crystal one time to the right, once to the left, and one last time to the right. Then set the crystal down in front of the candle.

4. Take your salt and make a circle around the candle and crystal in a clockwise direction. As you are sprinkling your salt, say this potent incantation three times: "I am safe. I am protected."

5. Imagine an iridescent white light surrounding you and the thing or space that you are protecting, cleansing and letting go of anything that is not needed. Imagine this light hardening into a sparkly black shield that will reflect back anything that is not for your highest good.

6. Let your candle burn all the way down. You can use a birthday candle for faster burning if you do not have a lot of time. Make sure you don't leave the candle unattended; extinguish the flame if you are not around.

7. Leave your spell set up for three days. When the three days are over, collect the salt from the circle and sprinkle it around the space that you want to protect or dispose of it in nature. Keep your crystal on you for protection, as it has now been supercharged with Crystal Enchanter magic.

———

Being protected physically, energetically, and spiritually as you continue to explore your Crystal Enchanter magic is essential to your practice. Being aware of what you are thinking and the intentions that you are setting daily are key to staying protected and feeling supported. Negative energies and emotions cannot attach themselves to you if you are high-vibing and focusing on your goals and your visions instead of focusing on what is lacking. These healing crystals are here to share their magic with you and to enhance the energy of protection, but it all starts with you. Creating a positive mindset and working on clearing your energetic field can help you stay grounded, focused, and protected. A Crystal Enchanter knows that all magic starts with thoughts, words, and actions. Keep practicing, and know that you will always be protected by your crystals if you focus on joy and love.

Chapter 11
Crystal Grids

Crystal grids are powerful magical tools for a Crystal Enchanter to use when you want to amplify the power of manifestation for your intentions. They are also a gorgeous way to bring your dreams into reality and to connect your thoughts to the physical world. The potent power that can be created with a crystal grid comes from the combined energies of the crystals laid out in a unique way that is tuned in with your intention. Using one crystal for manifesting is terrific, but merging the energy of a bunch of stones to create a pattern and design of sacred geometry can boost your magic ten times or more! You can create a crystal grid for any intention and any goal very quickly.

During my sacred crystal visualizations journeying into Atlantis, I was shown how technology was created with crystals and how these precious stones were used as the primary energy source for everything that they did, especially healing. Imagine crystals explicitly placed in the cities and palaces of Atlantis to channel energy for protection and crystals embedded in their clothing in a specific pattern for healing and manifesting. All this was to work with the designs and placement of the crystals to maximize their healing powers and to create a vortex of energy that was charged with intention. That is the very definition of a crystal grid.

Now, a lot of my clients were intimidated by the thought of creating a crystal grid at first. And actually, so was I. In the past, I thought my crystal grid had to look like the intricately designed crystal grids that I saw posted online. The more I cultivated my Crystal Enchanter practice, I realized that crystals are fluid and working with them is very intuitive. There is no "right" way to work with crystals because as long as you feel good and have fun, then they will be happy to work with you. Creating crystal grids empowers the crystals to work synergistically so that they magnify the energies of each other.

Just like how your crystals choose you, the gems for your crystal grid will come together magically on their own. You might suddenly "find" a crystal out of nowhere when you are collecting tools for your grid. It may seem random, but it's not. Learn to trust your intuition when you are creating. That is how I create my most potent healing grids; I follow the crystals and see which ones feel or look right to me when I am creating the grid. You can start by gathering crystals that match the energies of your intention, but if a random crystal feels like it needs to be there and the meaning doesn't entirely match your intention, put it in the grid anyway.

If you have no idea what you are doing but the crystal grid looks pretty to you, then your work is done! You don't have to create a perfect sacred geometric shape for your grid to work. It is about your intention and belief. The crystals and the grid itself are just extra tools to help you focus on manifesting your thoughts into reality.

Sacred Geometry Symbols

When looking into crystal grids, more often than not, you will come across sacred geometry. Many crystal grid practitioners like to incorporate sacred geometry symbols in their grids because these enchanted shapes can amplify the magic and focus of a grid. The Universe is a combination of five sacred geometry shapes, also known as the *platonic solids*. These shapes were named after the ancient Greek philosopher Plato, not because he discovered them, but because he wrote about them in a work called *Timaeus*. These five sacred shapes are the tetrahedron, hexahedron, octahedron, dodecahedron, and icosahedron. Plato wrote how each of these shapes resonate with a magical element: earth, fire, water, air, and spirit. All the platonic solids are congruent, having the same number of faces that meet at the vertices and equal sides and angles. Everything can be traced back to these platonic solids, from animals and plants to human DNA and cell structure.

Since ancient times, mystics and spiritual teachers have applied meaning to these shapes. It is believed that in these shapes, sacred geometry, were the secret to life. You are sacred geometry. This book is sacred geometry. Everything you ingest, touch, see, and come into contact with is sacred geometry. Sacred geometry is the universal language of creation. It is a mathematical formula that shapes the Universe and its dimensions. The core of all things has a mathematical code that influences and informs how it should appear to be in the physical reality. Sacred geometry reminds us that we are an integral part of the whole, and we are all one.

When looking to create a crystal grid with sacred geometry, it is important to understand what each of the shapes represent. Here is a brief guide to three of my favorite powerful sacred geometry symbols, the meanings, and how you can use them to supercharge your crystal grid magic.

The Flower of Life

You may see the Flower of Life, a sacred geometric shape, carved into crystals or tattooed on someone. It is created of multiple evenly spaced, overlapping circles placed in a flower pattern. The Flower of Life has sixfold symmetry, similar to that of a hexagon. There is a belief that a secret symbol is held within the Flower of Life, a symbol that holds the most sacred patterns of the Universe. The

Flower of Life is not one of the platonic solids, but it does embody the energy of creation, of you, and of everything in the Universe.

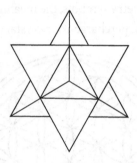

Merkaba

This sacred geometric shape is not one of the five platonic solids either, but it is known as a three-dimensional star of sacred truth and eternal wisdom.[5] The root meaning of Merkaba is derived from the Hebrew word *Merkava*, which means "chariot." The magical workings of this sacred geometry can be used to activate a higher frequency in the human body and enhance your life force.[6]

....

5. Frazier, *Crystals for Beginners*, 41.

6. Hall, *The Ultimate Guide to Crystal Grids*, 86.

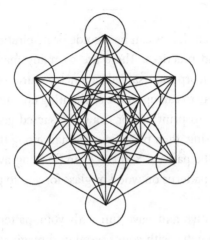

Metatron's Cube

Metatron's Cube is named after Archangel Metatron, who is connected with the flow of energy in creation. This sacred geometric shape contains many geometric shapes, including but not limited to the Star of David, the circle, the Merkaba, and the cube.[7] You can find all five platonic solids hidden inside Metatron's Cube, just like how these sacred patterns are hidden within the Universe. This magical symbol can help you alchemize negative thoughts into positive ones and connect with your higher self and the divine.

....

7. Lazzerini, *Crystal Grids Power*, chap. 3.

These sacred shapes can be a guide or inspiration to your crystal grid practices. There are so many magical ways you can incorporate sacred geometry into your magic. An easy way to call upon the enchanting energies of these symbols is to print out or draw the sacred geometry of your choosing, then place your crystals along the lines or spaces of the pattern. You can even find engraved sacred geometric patterns on wood or glass for you to place your grid upon.

Be creative and have fun with your patterns. Using sacred geometry with your crystal grid magic is optional. Whatever shape you create, know that your crystal and you are already filled with the magic of these patterns. Rules for creating crystal grids: *There are no rules.*

Magical Tools for Creating a Crystal Grid

Let me share a Crystal Enchanter secret with you that many people don't know. When creating a crystal grid, you can use more than just crystals! Using other magical tools can add another element to your manifesting and enhance the energies that you are calling in. In this section, I will be sharing a variety of magical tools that you can incorporate to create a more powerful grid.

Everything in this section is optional! You can use items that aren't included in this section if you feel called to do so. Pick and choose what is calling to you. When selecting your tools, you should feel happy and joyful. Each item should feel like it belongs. If you aren't vibing with a certain crystal, change it up, even if that crystal's meaning is what you supposedly need in the grid. Do it your way, and your crystal grid will rock it.

Crystals, Of Course!

Choose some magical sparkly crystals for your grid—big ones, small ones, just go crazy. I like to make my grid patterned, so I choose an even number of the same shape or type of crystal so that my grid will be symmetrical.

I like to put a larger crystal in the center of the grid and imagine all the other crystal energies synced up and shooting my intention into the Universe with love. Using a larger tower with the crystal tip pointed up works well for me.

If you do not have access to any crystals, you can still create a magical grid. Just skip on outside and collect some rocks. Crystals and stones are both part of the mineral kingdom. Rocks are free, and they can be just as magical as crystals.

A Crystal Activation Wand

This can be a natural crystal of any kind that you use to activate your crystal grid. It should be at least two to three inches in length, and it can be however wide you would like. Make sure that this activation wand has one pointed side and that the other side has a flat or rounded end. This is because the wand will be sending energy outward. You are directing your intention into the crystal grid with the tip of the pointed crystal.

A Small Piece of Paper

You can use this to write your intention or goal on. You could also choose to put this under your center crystal.

A Sacred Space to Place the Grid

Find a place in your home where you would like to place your grid. Choose someplace where it will not be disturbed by other people or your cute animals.

A Crystal Grid Cloth or Engraved Wood with Sacred Geometry

There are many items like this that you can find online or in stores. Again, you don't have to have a grid cloth or engraved wood. These are optional. However, I find that they magnify the intention and energy.

Flowers, Leaves, Feathers, or Anything that You Find in Nature

These can enhance the energy of your grid. One time I stepped outside of my house and found an already-dead bee right before creating my grid. It was a gift from the

Universe, and it felt right to add it to my grid, so I did! It really is about whatever means something to you.

Candles

You can choose candles using color magic to boost the energy of your crystal grid. Light them during the creation of the grid and extinguish them when you are finished. Every time you charge your grid, relight the same candles again. I love adding candles to my magical practices because they help me "fire up" my energies.

Essential Oils

These are also a fantastic magical tool to add to your crystal grid. When working with essential oils, remember to always dilute them with a base oil like coconut oil. You can match the energy of the oil to the energy of your intention and anoint your crystals before you add them to the grid. Drop a little bit of the diluted essential oil on your hands and gently rub the oil onto your crystals as you send the crystal love and good vibes. A little goes a long way—do not drench the crystal in the oil.

Tarot or Oracle Cards

These can be used in your crystal grid as a focus tool. Select a card that represents the energy that you are calling in. Make sure this is an energy that can support your intention. You can put your chosen card above the crystal grid, in the middle of it, or under the center crystal. For example, if I intend for a loving relationship, I would select the Two of Cups from my tarot deck to use as focused energy. If I am calling in money and prosperity, I would use the Nine of Pentacles in my crystal grid.

Crystal Grid Instructions

In previous sections, I shared ideas for the shape of your grid and other magical items you can incorporate, but know that a simple pattern of stones in any shape will work. It's all about your intention and focus! That is what empowers your grid. As long as you have that, you are good as gold. The following are some basic instructions for creating your crystal grid.

Create Your Intention

Before you create your crystal grid or select any crystals for it, it is essential to have a purpose to focus the energy on. Let your intention be specific. Write down all the details. Make this intention as complex or as simple as you choose, but make sure it is believable to you, meaning it is something that you can make happen in your life. What intentions are you looking to manifest? Are you looking to attract a loving, trusting partner? Are you wanting to bring abundance and wealth to your business? Maybe getting a good night's sleep is something you are focused on, or perhaps you want to activate your third eye and connect intimately with your intuition. You can use any intention for your crystal grid as long as you believe it's possible.

Choose Your Crystals

Now that you know what your intention is for your crystal grid, it is time to search for your magical gems. (If you do not have access to crystals, remember you can always just use rocks.) Use this book as a guide to select crystals with the same vibrational energy as your intention, or just grab the crystals that feel right for your grid.

As described previously, I like to choose one large center crystal and use smaller crystals for the patterns around it. If you are going to make a symmetrical crystal grid, be aware of what crystals you are choosing, even if you are letting your intuition guide you. There are no right or wrong crystals; just find ones that make you happy. Trust in your magic.

Cleanse Your Sacred Space

The space that you choose to create your crystal grid in should have happy vibes. It should be a place that is sacred to you. Clean the space physically and then use herbal smudge wands, sage, or your inner light to clear any negative, stale energies in the space.

Write Your Intention on a Small Piece of Paper

Place the paper with your intention on it in the middle of the grid under your center crystal. This step is optional, but I like to do this because it brings my thoughts into physical reality even more. If you don't do this step, your grid will still be just as powerful—I've had manifestations come true both ways—but I highly recommend it.

Center Yourself

Take three deep breaths in and out to help you center yourself. When you feel centered, say your intention aloud. Then visualize your intention as if it is happening already and has become a reality. Step into it and allow all of your senses to experience it fully. The more vivid and detailed your visualization is, the more you will empower your intention.

Place Your Crystals in a Pattern

As you come out of your visualization, hold on to that energy and start placing your stones in a pattern. You can have the pattern planned out in advance, or you can let your intuition guide you and see where the stones would like to be placed. This part is my favorite; I go into a meditative state and let my hands flow, creating, enabling the stones to guide me wherever they choose to be. Take your time, but don't get stuck on having the grid be perfect.

Make sure you hold on to your intention as you put every crystal in its place.

Activate Your Grid

Now that your crystals are in their most potent position and you are happy with your crystal grid, it is time for the activation! Grab your trusty crystal activation wand and aim the pointed end of the wand at a smaller stone on the outer edge of your grid. For those of you that do not have a wand, you can simply point your dominant hand's pointer finger for this step.

You can start with any crystal. I like to start at the top and go clockwise. You will be tracing the crystals like you are connecting invisible dots. Using your wand as the pen, you are activating and combining the energies of all the crystals to create one big vortex of power, infused by you and your intention.

Sending Out Your Visualization

When you have finished connecting all the crystals with your wand, imagine the center crystal shooting a beam of sparkly light into the Universe, sending your intention and visualization with love.

Congrats! Toss some Unicorn confetti! You have super-charged your crystal grid, and your intention is on its way to becoming reality. Now all you have to do is let it go, clear your thoughts, and believe. Take a deep breath in and notice if you have any questions about how or when this will happen. Take another breath in and let it all go.

For two days, forget about what you just did. Do other magical stuff. Don't think about your intention. After two days, start creating a plan that will help you achieve your goal, including smaller steps you can take to help you. Take three aligned actions every day to get you one step closer to your goal. By doing so, you will know that you are doing your part, and the Universe will deliver your intention in divine timing.

To maximize the energy of your crystal grid, I suggest you leave the crystal grid out for at least forty days. Forty days is a magical, transformative amount of time that is used in many traditions and cultures. For example, according to Kundalini Yoga, it takes forty days to change any habit. It takes this amount of time to reprogram your mind and nervous system, and this time allows you to integrate a new habit into your whole being. In Judaism, there is a sacred practice of repenting for forty consecutive days. And the Christian tradition of Lent is a forty-day tradition of fasting and prayer. So as you can see, forty days is used in many practices. It doesn't matter if you even believe in the power of this number or not; it works if you just do it. At the end of the forty days, magical shifts happen! I like to keep my crystal grid out for a little bit longer so that I can continue to call in high vibes and to integrate this new energy into my life.

Don't just stop at one crystal grid. Create more around your home for ultimate high vibes all around! There are infinite possibilities available for you at every moment, and anything can happen for you. Don't live life by chance. Be clear about what you want to call in and use the magic within you to manifest your best life. Crystal grids can help you triple your manifesting powers and work together with you to shift your life immediately. What would usually take a year to achieve might manifest in months, and what would ordinarily take months might happen in days. Crystal grids are not just gorgeous decorations—they are a powerful magical tool for a Crystal Enchanter.

Crystal Tip
Combine the Magic

Combining the magic you've learned in this book is truly the ultimate mission for a Crystal Enchanter. Use what resonates with you and what works for you, then leave the rest. However you create your magical crystal practice is perfect for you. There is no right or wrong way to cultivate your Crystal Enchanter craft, as there is only *your* way.

With that being said, when performing a spell, you can easily incorporate crystal grids into your work. Get creative with what you have and what your intuition is guiding you to do. Why not combine these magical modalities and create quantum shifts in your life? Everything that you learn in this book can be mixed and matched harmoniously to create even more enchantment in your life.

EXERCISE
Crystal Grid Art

If you are now obsessed with crystal grids and want to take them to the next level, then this magical exercise is for you. I am introducing you to crystal grid art!

You can make crystal grid art to hang around your house, or you could even start your own business and sell your art. Follow the same steps as you would to create a crystal grid in your space. The only difference is that, instead of laying your grid on a cloth or piece of wood, you glue your crystal grid onto a canvas or inside a box frame. E6000 permanent craft adhesive works great for this.

This way, you have a magical crystal grid always hanging on your wall, permanently filling the room with good energy!

Chapter 12
Crystal Potions

Safe Crystal Potions Practice: Before creating any crystal potion that will be inhaled, absorbed into your body, or ingested in any way, please research the crystal to see if it is toxic or harmful. If you are putting crystals into water, first check to see if the crystal is water safe. If it is not or if you are unsure, create your potions with the indirect method shown in this chapter. If you are using the direct method to create a potion, first cleanse your crystal by using soap and water or by boiling the crystal in hot water.

———

Crystals are sparkly, gorgeous, and fun to work with, and to bring even more of their energies into your

225

life, you can create crystal potions. Crystal potions absorb the vibrational pattern, energy, and unique signature of a crystal, infusing the water with its magic. In this chapter, I will share with you two ways of infusing crystal energy into water: a direct and an indirect method. We will then dive into pairing essential oils with crystals for amplification of energies in your crystal potions. I'll also be sharing one of my favorite techniques for crystal potions, which is to create sprays that can be used to alchemize your energy and the energy of the room.

The actual science of how crystal potions work is still a mystery, but they were created by ancient cultures for thousands of years. Water itself is exceptionally magical. All living creatures need water to survive, the earth is covered by water, and the human body is made up of water. The element of water is healing and cleansing. Many beliefs and religions use water to bless people, even today. Water can absorb emotions, energy, and anything in its surroundings. This makes water the perfect tool to infuse with the healing frequencies of crystals; it holds and amplifies crystal energies.

By the end of this chapter, you will be able to blend your own potent crystal potions for daily use. You may think that creating crystal potions is a long and complicated process, but it's simple. As you begin experimenting with crystal potions, try creating your potions in different ways and take notes in your Crystal Enchanter spell book about the process and its outcome. Then you can see which methods resonate with you the most and create the best results.

Two Methodologies of Creating Crystal Potions

There are two methods you can implement to create your crystal potions—the direct method and the indirect method. The direct method is when your potion is created by putting the crystal into the water during the process. The indirect method is used when you know your crystal is toxic or harmful, when your crystal is not water safe, or when you are unsure if your crystal is toxic or harmful. The indirect methods allows you to infuse your potion without the crystal ever touching the water. Before you start on your potions, research your crystals and any other magical ingredients going into your concoction. Then decide which method is best for your brew.

Both methods for brewing your potions are equally powerful and magical. To craft a potent magical blend, follow these steps:

Direct Method

Use this magical method if you know your crystal is water safe and nontoxic. This method is perfect for crystal potion sprays, face and body washes, or altar offerings.

1. Select a crystal that resonates with the energy you would like to embody. Charge your crystal in the moonlight (or sunlight) for positive healing energies and to cleanse it of any negative energies. Then physically cleanse the crystal with soap and water.

2. Place your selected crystal in a glass cup, water bottle, or pitcher. Fill your glass container with filtered water.

3. Activate your crystal potion by imagining the crystal's energy sparkling and infusing itself into the water. State your intention and what you want the crystal to help you with.

4. Let the crystal integrate with the water for at least one hour before you use the potion in your Crystal Enchanter practice.

Indirect Method

This method should be used if you are unsure about the safety of your crystal, know you have a crystal that is toxic or breaks down in water, or if you are just germophobic. I always use the indirect method, especially if I am ingesting the potion. When in doubt, use the indirect method.

1. Select a crystal that resonates with the energy you would like to embody. Charge your crystal in the moonlight (or sunlight) for positive healing powers. Energetically cleanse your crystal of negative energies before you start.

2. Select a smaller glass container with a lid, like a glass jam jar, and a bigger glass container that the smaller container will fit inside. Sanitize both containers with boiling water before use.

3. Place your crystal in the smaller glass container so that it will not directly touch the water that you will be consuming. Seal the smaller glass container, then place it in the bigger glass container.

4. Fill the bigger glass container with filtered drinking water.

5. Activate your crystal potion by imagining the crystal's energy sparkling and infusing itself into the water. State your intention and what you want the crystal to help you with.

6. Let the crystal integrate with the water for at least one hour before you use the potion in your Crystal Enchanter practice.

Infusing your water with the magic of the crystal to create a powerful potion is that simple. In the next two sections of this chapter, I will share with you a couple of ways to use your crystal potion.

Always be intentional and mindful when you are creating your crystal potions. Also, a good Crystal Enchanter practice to have when making crystal potions is to smile. Smiling will put you in a good mood and infuse good vibes into your potions.

Crystal Potion Water

I have found crystals to be more powerful when the gems touch the skin. Now, imagine crystal energy circulating throughout your entire body, through every cell and the bloodstream, and how much more magical that would be. You would literally be embodying crystal energy in the physical realm. This is 100 percent possible with crystal potions! This type of crystal potion is also known as gem water, crystal tonic, gem elixir, crystal essence, and more. Whatever it is called, they all refer to the same magical practice of infusing your water with the healing energies of the crystals and then ingesting that water. Drinking crystal potion water is said to be more potent than just wearing the gems on your body or having them around in the room. However, we all react to crystal magic differently, so you will have to decide that for yourself.

Since this type of crystal potion will be taken into the body, it is vitally important that you make sure it is safe for humans and Crystal Enchanters to consume. You have to be careful when selecting stones because some crystals dissolve or rust in water. Also, some crystals contain minerals that are toxic and poisonous, so they are not safe to be ingested. If you'd like to use the direct method, use crystals like clear quartz, rose quartz, and smoky quartz, which are safe to infuse directly in water. Actually, any natural quartz crystal can be used to brew your crystal potion water through the direct method. Before you use the direct method, I recommend cleansing your crystals thoroughly with soap and water or sanitizing them first in boiling water, as crystals have pores and crevices that can be filled with germs and bacteria. Please do your research on crystals and make sure what you are drinking is safe. With all of that being said, the safest way to create crystal potion water is through the indirect method.

Once you have clean, safe crystals for your crystal potion water, follow either the direct or indirect method to create your magical brew. (Use the direct method if you are absolutely sure that the crystal is safe to ingest. Use the indirect method for crystals you know are unsafe for direct infusion and ingestion. Always use the indirect method if you are unsure.) After making your crystal potion water and allowing it to sit for at least an hour, drink it. Did you notice that the water tastes fresher and cleaner? Did it create tingles in your body as you drank it? That is a sign that your intention and the crystal energy have been infused in your water and are now filling you up with magic.

If you are new to the Crystal Enchanter path and don't feel anything different, don't worry! Just trust that the potion is working. Keep practicing and brewing your crystal potions to get used to connecting with crystal energies. One magical day, you will notice the difference and suddenly remember what you have just read in this book. That day might not be today. It might not even be next week. But when that day comes, you will know it. Cheers to enchanting your water!

Crystal Potion Spray

Note: Crystal potion sprays should never be ingested, even when using the indirect method.

Using a crystal potion as a spray is an energy-enhancing tool that you can add to your Crystal Enchanter practice. By merely spraying the crystal potion around the room or on yourself with intention, you can take your magic to the next level. And, as an extra bonus, crystal potions will make your room smell amazing.

You can buy crystal potion sprays online, but I highly recommend crafting your crystal potion sprays yourself because you can empower the spray with your energy and sprinkle in a dash of your magic. Doing it yourself will also create a more powerful crystal potion spray for your collection than those you buy from the store.

The following crystal potion spray can be used to enhance the energies of a room and your personal energy. With this magical spray, you will have the option to incorporate essential oils to amplify the energy even more. If you're not sure which essential oil to choose, there is an entire section on essential oil and crystal pairings later in this chapter.

How to Create a Crystal Potion Spray

1. Decide what type of energy and magic you want to embody or call in. Choose a small crystal (or group of small crystals) that holds the energy that you have selected. Make sure the crystal(s) can fit into a glass spray bottle. Storing your potion in a glass bottle will allow your spray to last longer.

2. Cleanse and charge your crystal(s), then add them to your crystal potion spray bottle. If you are not sure if a crystal is water safe, if you are using a crystal that does not do well in water,

or if you are using a crystal that is harmful, use the indirect method to infuse the water first instead of adding the crystal(s) directly to the bottle.

3. Fill your glass spray bottle almost to the top with distilled water. Then, if you wish to infuse your spray with essential oils, choose ones that have the energy you desire to create and drop them into your bottle. I recommend about twenty-five to thirty drops per each eight-ounce bottle. In addition, to keep the crystal potion fresh, some people add unscented alcohol or witch hazel during this step. I normally skip these two ingredients in my potions because I tend to use up all my spray pretty fast.

4. Leave your bottle out in the moonlight to charge. You can leave it out during the new moon for beginnings, wishes, and manifestations or under the full moon for healing, cleansing, and protection. This step is optional, and you may charge your potion during any lunar phase (or even in the sun, if you wish). Do whatever feels healing and magical for you.

5. Activate your crystal potion by sharing your intention with your spray before use. Imagine your crystal and essential oil sparkling bright in the water, infusing it with magical energy. Make sure you give your crystal spray a gentle shake before you use it so that the essential oil is mixed thoroughly with the water before spraying. Every time you spray the potion, do so with intention by saying what you would like to feel. This will bring even more positive vibes into your space—and your reality.

After Care

If you used the indirect method, you will not have crystals inside the spray bottle. If you used the direct method and kept your crystals inside the spray bottle, take the crystals out after you have used up your crystal potion spray. You can clean them with soap and water and reuse them in your next spray, or you can keep them with you for good vibes.

EXERCISE
Magical Ways to Use
Your Crystal Potion Spray

Cleanse the energy of the room. Whenever you feel the air is stuffy or weighed down, it is time for a cleanse. You can also use your spray after you've had guests over to clear their energy out.

Spray after a disagreement or fight to change the residual energy that was left in the room into something positive and uplifting.

Use a calming and relaxing crystal potion spray on your linens or pillows to help you rest peacefully throughout the night.

Crystal Enchanter magic practitioners often use potions and spray before, during, or after rituals, ceremonies, and spells.

To be in a high vibe all day, spray some crystal potion on your clothes so that you are wearing—and are covered in—magic. Immerse the energy of the enchanted potion into your aura.

Spray some frankincense and lavender crystal potion in your hair to promote healthy growth. This is also a great mixture to freshen up after coming home from a smoky place. Make sure to blow dry your hair with cold air first to get out most of the smoke.

Spray a prosperity crystal potion in your wallet to manifest a positive flow of money coming into your life. Claim your abundance!

Spray your car for protection—especially your tires, if you pop them a lot like me. During this process, I also like to call upon my guides, Unicorns, and angels for safe travels.

Spray your crystals and any divination objects, like tarot cards, to cleanse and reset the energy of the items.

Before you give a gift to someone, spray the present with a high-vibe crystal potion. The person receiving your gift will feel the positive energy as they open up the offering.

Spray your packages before you send them out. This will protect them and help make sure that they get to their destination swiftly.

Essential Oil and Crystal Pairings

Note: Any crystal potions brewed with essential oils are not safe for ingestion. Never ingest essential oils.

Before we move on to creating crystal potion sprays, let us first look at the magic that essential oils can bring to your potions. The essential oil and crystal pairing will come in handy when brewing your enchanted sprays.

Like crystals, essential oils are harvested from the earth and have potent healing abilities. Using the oils can shift your energy, emotions, and even your mood. From my personal experience, I know that these magical tools truly shift your energies. I've experimented and had aura photos taken while holding crystals with and without essential oils. The pictures with crystals and essential oils paired together showed that my aura was more radiant and even showed up as different colors.

Adding essential oils to your crystal potions is optional, but crystals seem to vibrate with joy when paired up with essential oils. They are like BFFs. Mixing essential oils and crystals in your crystal potion sprays or spells will amplify the magic you are calling in. Similar to crystals, each essential oil element vibrates on a particular frequency. Select the crystal and essential oil that vibrate on the same energetic level you are choosing to embody. You can then use these tools to create a potent crystal potion spray that can help you manifest your intentions at a multidimensional level.

When selecting essential oils, make sure that you have researched the brand and company. Even though you are not ingesting your potion, essential oils should still be chosen with care. They should be certified pure therapeutic grade and gathered ethically. The FDA does not regulate essential oils, so any company can put "100 percent pure" or "organic" on the bottle, but that doesn't mean it is true. Do your own research online and see which brand aligns with your beliefs. Make sure the product is safe to use and that you connect with it. Go with your intuition! Whatever essential oil you choose will be perfect for your potion.

Included in the next section is an essential oil and crystal pairings guide for the different energies that we talked about in chapters 5 through 10. These pairings are just a guide to help you get started while creating enchanting crystal potion blends, so feel free to add more magical ingredients or to switch them out.

Magical Oil Warning

Pets are more sensitive to essential oils, so if you have pets, please do your research before diffusing essential oils or spraying them into the air. There are some oils that are more dangerous than others; for example, tea tree essential oil is harmful to dogs and cats. However, keep in mind that every pet is different and may be harmed by certain oils.

If you have pets and are using essential oils, make sure that you leave the door open while spraying or diffusing so that your pet may leave if they do not like the scent. Also make sure to keep the area well ventilated.

One resource is *Essential Oils for Pets: Ultimate Guide for Amazingly Effective Natural Remedies for Pets* by Alexander Huffington. It is best to consult your veterinarian before using any potions containing essential oils on your pets.

Crystal Potion Blends for Love and Relationships

Pairing the following essential oils and crystals will infuse a room with the energy of love and will boost good vibes in your relationships.

Rose + Morganite

Roses are the most popular flower associated with love. Roses are a common flower that lovers get for each other. So, if you are looking for romance, rose essential oil can bring you just that. Its romantic scent can conjure up feelings of love and desire. The floral essence is strong, so you only need a few drops. Rose essential oil is a bit on the pricey side, but if you do decide to splurge, it is magical and totally worth it. Combine rose essential oil and morganite to brew a royal VIP crystal potion of unconditional love, meant to attract your ideal lover.

Jasmine + Garnet

Jasmine has been used for love and relationships for years because of its aphrodisiac magic. This exotic scent can stir up your libido and get you in the right mood. Create a sexy scented crystal potion with jasmine essential oil and a garnet gem to ignite passion in the bedroom.

Ylang Ylang + Rose Quartz

Ylang ylang essential oil also has aphrodisiac properties. It can arouse the sensual side of you with its tantalizing scent and balance your emotions at the same time. Brew a crystal potion with ylang ylang essential oil and rose quartz to have an adventurous and fun night with your partner.

Crystal Potion Blends for Prosperity and Money

Ready to claim your wealth and prosperity? These three essential oil and crystal pairings will boost the abundant energies in your crystals.

Wild Orange + Citrine

Wild orange essential oil is the oil of prosperity and abundance. The citrusy scent is also very welcoming. It's one of my favorite oils to use in a spray. Wild orange can boost your energy and help you stay motivated. Mix this magical oil with citrine to brew a happy, joyful, and abundant crystal potion.

Ginger + Pyrite

Magnify your abundant energetic frequency with ginger essential oil. Ginger will dispel any negative thoughts or beliefs you have about money and wealth and can release doubts and worries about prosperity. Create a crystal potion with ginger essential oil and pyrite crystal to call in abundance.

Black Pepper + Tiger's Eye

Just like black crystals, black pepper essential oil can help repel negative energy and create a vortex of abundance around you. Infusing black pepper with the tiger's eye crystal can create a powerful, money-manifesting crystal potion that is also very protective. I would suggest adding lemongrass or cedar wood essential oil to this combination as well because black pepper essential oil does not smell too great on its own.

Crystal Potion Blends for Health and Well-Being

Although all essential oils have different healing properties, here are three essential oil and crystal pairings for overall health and well-being.

Peppermint + Lepidolite

Peppermint essential oil not only alleviates headaches and tension, but it can also boost your energy level and awaken your senses. Using the indirect method, create a powerful crystal potion with peppermint essential oil and lepidolite to enhance and promote emotional health.

Eucalyptus + Malachite

Use eucalyptus essential oil to invite positive health and well-being energy into your life. Eucalyptus can reduce anxiety and tension you are feeling and replace it with a calming yet energizing boost. Using the indirect method, brew a potent crystal potion that is purifying and healing with eucalyptus essential oil and malachite.

Frankincense + Clear Quartz

Frankie, as I call it, is also called the king of oils. If you aren't feeling well but do not know what ailment you have, grab frankincense essential oil because it can cure almost anything. This ancient oil is also a bit on the pricey side, but once you've experienced the magic of this oil you will want no other. Pair your frankie with clear quartz and create an epic healing crystal potion.

Crystal Potion Blends for Intuition and Psychic Powers

To connect with your intuition and gain spiritual clarity, incorporate these three essential oil and crystal pairings in your potion to amplify your psychic powers.

Melissa (Lemon Balm) + Labradorite

Melissa essential oil attracts high-vibrational energy for clarity and boosts happiness. This magical oil can help you radiate joy and sparkle brighter. Create a crystal potion with Melissa essential oil and labradorite to cheerfully tap into your intuitive magic and inner light.

Sandalwood + Fluorite

To gain clarity during devotional practices, ceremonies, rituals, and meditations, try using sandalwood essential oil. Sandalwood can help you connect with your higher self and intuition. Brew a crystal potion with sandalwood essential oil and fluorite to access your genius creativity and your connection with the divine.

Patchouli + Selenite

If you're seeking a calm focus that can help you stay attentive to your tasks, reach for patchouli essential oil. Patchouli is a fantastic oil for meditation. Using the indirect method, mix patchouli essential oil and selenite in your crystal potion to dive into the spiritual realm and receive the answers you are looking for.

Crystal Potion Blends for Peace and Calm

For a good night's rest or to simply have a moment of peace, brew a crystal potion with these three soothing essential oil and crystal pairings.

Lavender + Celestite

Lavender is known as the queen of oils, and it is one of the most popular essential oils around the world. It is widely recognized as a calming and soothing oil. The scent of lavender can instantly alleviate anxiety and depression. Brew a crystal potion with lavender essential oil and celestite to create a potent magical blend that can help you sleep and dream of angels.

Chamomile + Larimar

Chamomile is a gentle, calming oil that is well-known for its soothing qualities. This herb is often used in teas to reduce stress and anxiety. To wind down after a long, hard day and to experience a relaxing night, mix a crystal potion with chamomile essential oil and larimar and let the waves of relaxation wash over you.

Bergamot + Blue Calcite

Bergamot essential oil is often used as a mood booster when people feel stressed or anxious. This oil has a spicy citrus scent, and it smells even better when combined with lavender essential oil. Infusing bergamot with blue calcite in your crystal potion can help you chill out (while staying alert) throughout the day.

Crystal Potion Blends for Protection and Warding

For protection and warding in your private space or when you go out, create a crystal potion that repels negative energies with these three essential oil and crystal pairings.

Clary Sage + Black Tourmaline

Sage is a tool widely used to clear negative energy. Clary sage essential oil derives from the sage plant, so it does the same thing and is great for people who don't like the smell of burning sage. A crystal potion with clary sage and tumbled black tourmaline is the ultimate blend to get rid of low-vibrational energy and to protect and cleanse a space.

Lemongrass + Amethyst

This refreshing scent will brighten up your home and your energy. Lemongrass essential oil is used to release worries and clear negative vibrations. Amethyst is a beautiful warding stone. When you swirl lemongrass and amethyst together, this potion will create a protective shield around you so that only positive energies can enter.

Basil + Smoky Quartz

Basil is more than just another herb in your spice rack. It can also be a powerful essential oil that boosts your vibrational level so that you do not attract negative energies into your life. Both basil essential oil and smoky quartz are used for protection and warding. Brew a crystal potion using them to surround yourself with pure, abundant energy and to bless your space.

———

These Crystal Enchanter essential oil and crystal blends would be perfect to use to create your crystal potion sprays. There are many other ways you can use your blends. You could use the blends in anointing oil for candles or in magically infused beauty and healing products such as lotions and lip balm. Crafting and using a crystal potion spray is one of the easiest and most efficient ways of spreading the magic that you've brewed.

EXERCISE
Crystal Grid Potion

To super-duper charge your crystal potion, combine your potion ritual with a crystal grid. Whether you are creating a crystal potion spray or crystal potion water, you can add the element of crystal grids to your practice. Follow the magical instructions in chapter 11 to create a crystal grid around the glass container that is brewing your crystal potion. Doing so will magnify the crystal magic and your intention. You are letting the Universe know exactly what you desire and it will help you quantum shift your wishes into your reality.

Crystal Tip
Crystal Water Bottles

Currently, crystal water bottles are trending. Someone, a magical genius, finally created a water bottle with a real-life crystal embedded inside to infuse your water at all times. If you are looking for an easy way to create your crystal potions, then this is the way to go. The crystals that are selected for water bottle use are nontoxic, which makes drinking healing water a breeze. There are many magical brands online with amazing prices, so you can choose the one that is perfect for you. They even have crystal water bottles with a tea infuser!

For some extra crystal water bottle magic, each time you refill your bottle and each time you take a sip, think of your intention and visualize the water infusing that energy into your body.

———

I hope brewing crystal potions will be a fun and magical practice that you add to your daily rituals. As you can see, there are many ways to work with crystals in our lives. The more you work with these enchanting gems, the more you will tune in to their energy. Your awareness of the crystals will intensify, and working with these magical minerals will become a habit. As you continue on your Crystal Enchanter journey, drink in the healing energies of these gems.

Chapter 13

How to Create Your Own Crystal Spells

Now that you've tried a couple of the spells that I have shared with you, you probably want to go deeper into your Crystal Enchanter practice and create your own. I encourage to do so because the spells you cast will be even more powerful than the ones I've shared. Your spells will embody your unique magic and energy.

Crafting your spells is almost effortless! You can create spells that work around your schedule, passions, and desires using the magical tools you have around you right this minute. You don't need to go out and buy extra items for your spells or rituals because you can use the things you already have in your home. I would suggest, though, that if there is something that keeps popping up in your mind that you feel you need for the magic to work, go out and get that thing. Trust your intuition.

There are no rules for creating spells. I will share my suggestions with you, but feel free to do what's right for you. Your spells will have your magic and your essence, so they do not need to be like any other spells you find on the internet or in books. You can continue to use the spells in this book to guide you if you feel called, but just do what's the most comfortable for you. With practice, you will figure out your magical formula for success. This is why you must have a Crystal Enchanter spell book: so that you will know what works and what doesn't work for you. Jot down your magical practices and reflect on each spell. In no time, you will be manifesting things into your life left and right!

Simple Guide to Creating Your Own Spells

1. Create your intention for the spell. Why are you doing this? What is your end goal? What do you want to achieve? What will you be calling in? What energies will you be working with?

2. Decide if you want to cast your spell on a special date to amp up the energy, like doing it on

the day of the full moon. Maybe you want to cast the spell under a new moon for new intentions. Choosing a special day is not required, but the extra energy can only help.

3. Gather your magical tools. Select items that could be symbols of your intention or could enhance the magic of your spell or ritual. Choose any object that relates to the energy around your intention. You can refer back to the sections in this book for guidance. Crystals and tarot cards are always easy to work with because each card and crystal has a specific energy and symbolism that you can use for your spells and rituals. Some other objects you can include are feathers, bells, rocks, paintings, herbs, figurines, flowers, and anything else that you feel represents your intention.

4. Write out the steps for your spell. There isn't a right or wrong way to do this. Start by finding your sacred space and tuning in. Usually, I like to release negative blocks or energies first. Then I call in my intention and desires to replace that empty space I have created. You can also just call in your intention without the release, if you'd like. Make sure you use every item on your magical tools list during your

spell, because you chose those items for a reason. I always include some kind of visualization in my craft because this is a potent tool for creating change.

5. Close out your spell by giving thanks to the Universe, your guides, or whoever you were working with. Closing the spell is very important because you don't want to leave that energy open. Saying thanks is an easy way to do so. You can also end your spell with affirmations such as "And so it is."

6. Journaling during or after your spell is encouraged.

7. Always keep magical tools such as herbs and candles in a safe place until your spell comes true. Once your spell manifests, you can either dispose of these types of items in your trash can (if the spell was for something positive and you called in energy) or throw them away in a trash can off of your property (if it was a spell to release something). If you worked with crystals, tarot cards, and other reusable magical tools, don't toss these out! Cleanse them and reuse them for your next spell.

"How Do I Know When a Spell Is Coming True?"

After finishing your spell, spend the next week looking for signs from your guides that your spell is working. This could include, but is not limited to: seeing magical numbers such as 11:11 on clocks, license plates, receipts, or social media; coming across items such as feathers, coins, or random physical items that mean good fortune or good luck to you; or seeing other people with the thing that you desire. For example, if you see a friend or someone around you receive the thing that you are manifesting, then you know your time is coming!

Within two to three weeks of initiating your spell, you should see progress or forward movement toward achieving your goal. If your spell was focused on manifesting a lover, you might meet this person, be introduced to this person, or have a date planned. If your spell was focused on manifesting money, you might see a job posting for a higher position. During this two-to-three week period after you cast your spell, make sure you are going out and taking action toward your intention.

In a few months, your spell should be fully realized and should have come true. Congratulations! If you do not see the success of your spell, go back to the drawing board. Think about what you need to change and do another spell. Maybe your energy was low on the day that you cast the spell, or perhaps you did not take appropriate action. Most of the time when a spell does not manifest, it is because of the intention you chose. Perhaps the intention you chose wasn't what you truly want, or maybe it wasn't clear enough about the desired outcome.

You can do different spells focused on the same intention in close succession, but do not do the same spell twice until at least one month later, even if you didn't receive messages or see movement during that time. You want to allow your spells to have the proper time to grow and be birthed. You will see that, more often than not, your spells manifest within the month if you allow yourself to trust, believe, and be open to the opportunities coming your way.

Crystal Tip
Spell Jar

Spell casting immediately begins when you are setting the space before you start the work. Depending on what spell, sometimes the casting even starts during the collection of my magical tools!

Creating a spell with a glass jar is one of my favorite ways to cast a spell. It is simple, easy, and very powerful. Most of the spells I cast are in my spell jar. I have one glass jar dedicated to spells, but you can have more than one. The glass jar I use is a medium-sized mason jar. Make sure whatever jar you get has a cover.

Between each spell, I wash my jar with water mixed with salt and then use herbal smudge wands to cleanse it. My glass jar is big enough to fit a tarot card and some crystals because those are magical tools that are consistent in my spells. If you do not have a jar big enough to hold a regular-sized tarot card, you could get a mini-sized tarot deck dedicated just for spells. You could also go online and print out a card image. That way, you can fold the paper so that it fits in your jar. If you are adding any herbs to your spell jar, like cinnamon, and you do not want to get your cards or crystals dirty, you can put the herbs in a small bag or wrap them up before putting them into your jar.

After you've filled your jar, put on the lid. I set a candle on top of the lid and let it burn out. I usually get a simple four-inch spell candle for this; you can buy these online. Four-inch spell candles take about forty-five minutes to burn out. If you want a candle that burns faster, you can buy a birthday candle. To make the candle stick to the lid so it doesn't fall over and become a fire hazard, I light the bottom of the candle to heat the wax before placing it on the lid. The wax will cool and harden, so the candle should stick to the lid and not move. Another option is to get a candle holder and to put the candle in it before settling that on top of the jar. Make sure to keep a close eye on the candle as it burns. Extinguish it if you have to leave the room.

There are so many ways to cast spells with spell jars, so try it out and see what resonates with you!

———

Go on now, Crystal Enchanter! Craft an amazing spell to manifest money, love, or health. Let your intuition guide you as you craft your magical practice. Focus on your desires and call them into your life intentionally. Not every spell will work. That is okay, because you will learn something valuable each time. Perhaps a failed spell is a lesson for you in your real life, or maybe it is a lesson in magic. Whatever happens, know that your wish will come to you in divine timing if you stay focused on what you desire. Keep a positive mindset, work on your energy, believe, and take aligned action.

You have all the knowledge and tools you need to create a life that you desire; spells will only increase your chances. Remember to start small if you are a newbie Crystal Enchanter. Cast spells that are fun and that will bring joy into your life. You don't need to try to solve a big problem that you are worried about right away; that can come later. The more you practice, the more confirmation you receive that your magic works, and the more your magic will increase. Build up your magic by practicing and crafting powerful spells, and have fun while doing it!

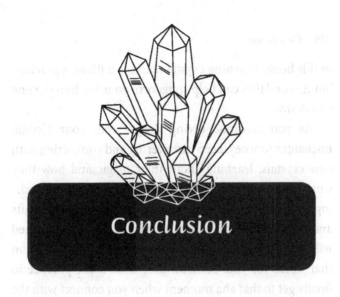

Conclusion

Even though we are now at the end of our journey in this book, I know that this is not the end of your Crystal Enchanter journey, but rather, hopefully, a beginning. Throughout this book, you've discovered different types of crystals for specific energies, how to connect with and activate crystals, and many enchanted ways to work with crystals in your magical practices. This is not a "read it once" type of crystal book that should be stored on your bookshelf. This book is meant to be something for you to continue to use and reference on your Crystal Enchanter path. When you need help finding the right crystal for your love spell, come back to this book. When you are ready to create your crystal potions, come back to this book. Learning crystal magic is a lifelong practice, but it is one that can help transform your life into the one you desire.

As you continue diving deeper into your Crystal Enchanter journey, keep discovering and connecting with new crystals, learning about their magic and how they work with you and for you. Keep journaling, researching, experimenting, and recording your magical crafts and results. Having a record of what you've accomplished will help you streamline your magic and create a system that works for you. Sometimes it takes some practice to finally get to that aha moment when you connect with the energy of the crystals or when your spell comes true. You will know when it happens to you, trust me! Then magic will seem effortless and natural, just like driving a car.

When you are confident enough, or when you feel called, the next step you can take to master your Crystal Enchantment is to share it with others. Share crystals with others, even if you don't feel comfortable talking about their crystal magic. As you feel more and more comfortable, share the magic with others also. You can even share this book! The truth is, the more you share the energy of the crystals, the more positive energy will come back to you.

To help you to regularly focus on good vibes coming into your life and to tap into the power of the crystals, here are some simple guidelines that I follow to keep myself aligned with my magic:

Crystal Enchanter Principles

1. Take care of your crystals and they will take care of you.

2. Have clarity about what you desire and then ask for it.

3. Allow, receive, and be present.

4. The Universe is your BFF.

5. Be kind to others and to yourself.

6. Spread sparkles, magic, and crystals.

7. Believe in magic and miracles.

8. Take aligned action every day.

9. Have an attitude of gratitude.

10. Whatever you send out will come back to you three times.

11. Your thoughts become reality.

12. Do things that make you happy.

13. Do no harm.

Most important of all, have fun with your crystals! Watch them sparkle, feel their magic as they heal you, and smile when you see them around your sacred space.

It has been my honor to guide you on your Crystal Enchanter path. My hope for you is that you are able to enjoy working with crystals as much as I have. I want you to live your best, five-star, magical life! Crystals truly are transformational.

I would love to continue to be a part of your Crystal Enchanter journey by celebrating your successes with you. When you post about your Crystal Enchanter practice, whether it is about this book or anything to do with crystals, tag me on Instagram (@pamelaunicorn) and use the hashtag #crystalenchanter so we can continue to share in this wonderful magic together!

See you around, magical Crystal Enchanter. Keep sparkling!

Bibliography

Chamberlain, Lisa. *Wicca Crystal Magic: A Beginner's Guide to Practicing Wiccan Crystal Magic, with Simple Crystal Spells*. Self-published, Chamberlain Publications (Wicca Shorts), 2015. Kindle.

Cunningham, Scott. *Cunningham's Encyclopedia of Crystal, Gem & Metal Magic*. St. Paul, MN: Llewellyn Publications, 1998.

Frazier, Karen. *Crystals for Beginners: The Guide to Get Started with the Healing Power of Crystals*. Berkeley, CA: Althea Press, 2017. Kindle.

Hall, Judy. *The Ultimate Guide to Crystal Grids: Transform Your Life Using the Power of Crystals and Layouts*. Beverly, MA: Fair Winds Press, 2017. Kindle.

Huffington, Alexander. *Essential Oils for Pets: Ultimate Guide for Amazingly Effective Natural Remedies for Pets*. Mind's I Books, 2015. Kindle.

Lazzerini, Ethan. *Crystal Grids Power: Harness the Power of Crystals and Sacred Geometry for Manifesting Abundance, Healing, and Protection*. Self-published, CreateSpace, 2017. Kindle.

Studeman, Kristin Tice. "Are You Obsessed with Crystals, Too? How Crystals Went from New Age Curiosity to Mainstream Sensation." *W Magazine*, January 24, 2017. https://www.wmagazine.com/story/crystals-go-mainstream-behind-the-crystal-healing-obsession/.

Index

To Write to the Author

If you wish to contact the author or would like more information about this book, please write to the author in care of Llewellyn Worldwide Ltd. and we will forward your request. Both the author and publisher appreciate hearing from you and learning of your enjoyment of this book and how it has helped you. Llewellyn Worldwide Ltd. cannot guarantee that every letter written to the author can be answered, but all will be forwarded. Please write to:

Pamela Chen
% Llewellyn Worldwide
2143 Wooddale Drive
Woodbury, MN 55125-2989

Please enclose a self-addressed stamped envelope for reply, or $1.00 to cover costs. If outside the U.S.A., enclose an international postal reply coupon.

Many of Llewellyn's authors have websites with additional information and resources.
For more information, please visit our website at
http://www.llewellyn.com.